IN GOD WE TRUST:

But Which One?

Best wishes,
Judith Hayes

A fresh, new look at the fatal flaws in religious belief

by Judith Hayes

FFRF, Inc.
PO Box 750
Madison WI 53701

Published by
Freedom From Religion Foundation, Inc.
PO Box 750
Madison WI 53701-0750
(608) 256-8900

First printing, September 1996

ISBN: 1-877733-11-3

Printed in the United States of America

To Susan,
a loving friend,
who unknowingly changed my life—
forever

Contents

Foreword

I wish I had had this book when I was struggling to hold on to my faith. I wouldn't have struggled so hard.

During those last few years I was preaching, I put on a face of confidence, as all ministers must do; but my clerical visage masked an underlying uneasiness and hypocrisy. I *told* everyone that I was speaking the truth, but did I *know* it? Not once, during my years of preaching, did anyone ever ask for my sources or evidences. No one suggested that the "good book" might be unreliable or dangerous, or that the arguments for the existence of God could be faulty. As long as I went unchallenged, my foundation for truth remained unexamined.

The subtitle of this book is "A fresh new look at the fatal flaws in religious belief." Thomas Paine's *The Age of Reason* has been enlightening us for more than two centuries with its incisive criticisms of the bible. Robert Ingersoll, Elizabeth Cady Stanton, and many other nineteenth-century freethinkers spoke clearly and forcefully about the fatal flaws of Christianity. Bertrand Russell's *Why I Am Not A Christian* and hundreds of twentieth-century voices have continued the healthy history of skepticism. But we are always in need of a fresh look — of something that speaks clearly and directly to *today's* believers.

What the world needs, before it becomes persuaded of the fatal flaws of belief, is not more criticism of religion — there is already enough there to convince even the least ambitious student that religions are houses built on sand. What the world needs is to "see" what's there.

When I first began sensing that Christianity might not be as sound as it sounds, I wish someone had taken me gently by the chin and turned my face, saying, "Look. Look over here."

This is exactly what Judith Hayes does. The scriptures have always had contradictions, but she helps us to *see* them. The unvarnished depictions of Jehovah and Jesus have not been hidden all these centuries — we just have to *look* at them.

If you are a freethinker, Judith's writings will give you a fresh perspective on how to apply religious criticism to the mind of a believer. This is the perfect book to give to your religious friends or relatives. Judith is a former insider who knows how to take believers gently by the chin.

If you are a believer, you will sense in these pages a ring of truth. This is not a wild cannon shot from a distant atheist pirate ship. This is an inspection of the inside of your own ship, an examination of the irreparable fissures in the hull of Christianity that are causing it to sink fast. Perhaps you will learn that the only way to be saved is to jump ship.

Judith Hayes has been writing for *Freethought Today* since 1994. Her clear, enjoyable columns (a few culled from this book) have received high praise from freethinkers around the continent. *In God We Trust: But Which One?* is a needed and welcome addition to the cause of freethought.

Dan Barker
Freedom From Religion Foundation, Inc.

Introduction

They say that God is everywhere. This has never been more true than today, in the 1990s. God is on our currency. He is invited to Congressional prayer breakfasts, public school graduation ceremonies and sporting events. These are trying times for those of us dedicated to the separation of church and state. Many states already have passed public school prayer laws and more are proposing them. Congress is considering a school prayer amendment and "creation science" is inching its way into public school science classes. James Madison would have been appalled.

There are those in the freethought community who frown on religious criticism, claiming it is a totally negative activity. That it is; but if Christians are going to try to push their Bible into our *public* classrooms, then it's time to take a good look at that Bible. The times demand it.

There have been hundreds of goddesses and gods worshipped throughout history. In the history of the United States, however, the Judeo-Christian tradition is by far the most familiar. This book will focus on that tradition, with particular emphasis on Christian fundamentalism. As you will see, the laws of logic unmask Christianity, exposing it as the empty theology that it is.

But those same laws of logic also apply to all other religions. Even though these other religions will not be examined here, they, too, cannot survive the rigors of intense scrutiny. When viewed through reason and not superstition, all religions fall by the wayside. They all emerge as dust in the wind, as the stuff that dreams are made of. As Walt Disney reminded us, "A dream is a wish your heart makes." A prayer is nothing more, no matter which god you believe you are addressing.

The Christian focus of this book would be considered alien to the point of being blasphemous in, for example, any Muslim country. And this underscores my whole point. If we want to discuss God, fine; but first we must state *which* god we're going to talk about.

Far too many freethought books are, in Mark Twain's phrase, chloroform in print. Scholarly treatises have their places, but very few of us can wade through them. So I'll leave the arcane analysis of metaphysics, epistemology, and eschatology (along with any attendant ontological arguments) to others.

This book is written in plain old English, and is intended for the average lay reader. If it causes anyone to pause and think — really think — about religion's role in society, it will have been worth the effort.

I think we all need to be reminded of the beautifully crafted *secular* Constitution that has been the bedrock of our successful democracy. May we never forget it.

1

Where Angels Fear To Tread

There is much in the Bible against which every instinct of my being rebels, so much that I regret the necessity which has compelled me to read it through from beginning to end. I do not think that the knowledge which I have gained of its history and sources compensates me for the unpleasant details it has forced upon my attention.

Helen Keller, *The Story Of My Life*

For the first twenty years of my life, the most important part *of* my life was my faith. Religion guided my every move. I was especially grateful, therefore, to have been born into a German Lutheran family, since everyone knew that Lutheranism was the One True Religion. (And we were Missouri Synod, which is as Lutheran as you can get.) I really felt that I had dodged a bullet here. What if I had been born (shudder) a Catholic; or, God forbid, an atheist?! Talk about *luck*.

So when I was around twelve and I formed a close friendship with a Japanese girl, I discovered to my horror that she was Buddhist. Can you imagine? Buddhist! This threw me into a tailspin. For one thing, I couldn't figure out how she could be so nice, being a Pagan and all. I was the original Goody Two Shoes, but Susan was actually nicer than *I* was. (She still is.) How could this be? But more important, I couldn't figure out how she was ever going to get into Heaven, where I, of course, was destined. Since I could not bear the thought of my best friend, Susan, spending eternity in Hell, I asked my religious leaders about this, and received a very complicated answer. I was told that she wouldn't necessarily go to Hell unless she had actually had the opportunity to accept Jesus Christ into her heart, and just having a Christian church next door to her home didn't necessarily mean that she ever really had the opportunity, and on and on. But it didn't satisfy me. And it didn't seem fair that just because I had been born into a certain family I was guaranteed a blissful eternity, whereas Susan's fate was far more dubious.

Thus was planted the seed of doubt, and as time went on my questions about Susan were treated first with stern impatience and finally with the abrupt command to forget about it. God would work it all out, and He didn't need any help from me. So I kept my doubts to myself. It still didn't seem fair, but I shut up about it. However, from that point on, I worried about it a great deal. Poor Susan.

My decision to read the entire Bible, and thereby shore up my faith and answer all of my nagging questions, was made with great trepidation. But my background for such an ambitious undertaking was certainly appropriate. My grandfather and my great-grandfather had both been Lutheran ministers. My father was the church organist and also taught Bible study classes. My mother was in the church choir (so was I) and my father read the Bible aloud every night after dinner. For one summer I actually taught vacation Bible school to the little kids. I was a voracious reader, and a better than average student. So even though I knew it would be arduous, I was certain that with enough time and effort I would emerge from my studies with a bright, untarnished faith. I couldn't have been more wrong.

I began my journey of discovery with the absolute determination of strengthening my faith. Just the opposite happened. I wanted to bolster my beliefs and to be able to back them up with quotations — chapter and verse if you will — but the further my studies took me, the less certain I became of *any* of my beliefs. I plunged even more fervently into my studies, which led to yet more doubts. I finally stopped going in circles and arrived at some inescapable conclusions. My own logical mind, which I felt certain would help me wade through the myriad of conflicting facts and see me safely to the other side of that sea of doubt, instead proved to be my undoing. I literally reasoned my faith out of existence.

Such a metamorphosis is not to be taken lightly and does not happen easily when your faith is very strong to begin with. I fought tooth and nail every step of the way. I wanted my faith, and felt I needed my faith, and watching it leave was a very wrenching experience. In a Bible study class, along with asking about my poor, damned friend Susan (after a while everyone in that class was tired of hearing about Susan), I also began asking very pointed questions about prayer and evil and the Pope.

The dusty responses I received were, I now realize, the result of simply not knowing how to answer such insightful questions. My questions were not of the smart-aleck variety, like so many of these kinds of questions are. No, my questions were prompted solely by the intense desire to understand. I needed to *know.* Alas, my religious leaders were not up to providing adequate answers to my heartfelt questions. So I set out on my own quest.

I understand now why the Catholic Church fought so hard to keep its Bible in Latin. If no one knows what it says, no one can question what it says. And almost *anything* sounds pretty in Latin. But a nitty-gritty English translation puts the Bible in a whole new, unflattering light. I'll bet there are many clergy who wish, very secretly of course, that they could have had a go at editing the Bible before the printing press had been invented. I'm sure they would like not to be faced with the anachronisms, the contradictions in the gospels, and the bloody violence that saturates the Old Testament. Yes, indeed, Latin is a pretty language.

None of these thoughts, however, was in my mind as I set out bravely to conquer this nemesis called Doubt. I remember my sad, little beginning as I plunged into Genesis, determined to learn the mysteries of life, the meaning of faith, and the reason why I was so miserable. I believed in God with all my heart, and with all my soul, and with all my mind. I was a very good girl. In my youth I had never once had to stay after school, and I can still remember clearly one of my few childhood lapses in behavior. After being told while shopping that, no, I could not eat one of those luscious-looking strawberries in the produce section, since it would be stealing, I went ahead and did it anyway when my mother wasn't looking. I was thereafter stricken with guilt and I prayed endlessly for forgiveness. I had been, almost literally, an angel of a child. So how could I possibly have wound up married to a tyrant? Why had God forsaken me? Everything in my religious training led me to believe that such a thing could not happen to those who put their trust in God. So I earnestly began the introspective process of examining my own trust.

After my eye-opening reading of the Bible I naturally went on to read other books about religion, and these other books finished the process that the Bible had started. These other books, written by nonbelievers, simply rang out with logic and clarity. My faith tottered and then collapsed as I found myself unable to resist the urgings of my own logical mind. The battle was over.

For a long time I missed my faith, since it seemed to simplify things, but overall its influence on my life was far more negative than positive. The helpless, put-your-trust-in-God attitude encouraged by religion is unhealthy and inimical to happiness, and undoubtedly was the major factor in my own early misery. The "trust in God" approach to life discourages critical thinking and skepticism, both of which you need in healthy doses to navigate this minefield called life. At the same time I also believe that no one who had anything to do with my religious training meant me any harm at all. (I cannot extend that same compliment to television evangelists, and I find their snake-oil approach to salvation revolting.)

Although I was confused for quite a while after my faith left,

I finally realized that there is a big, beautiful world out there, filled with promise, without a vengeful god or a pitchforked devil in sight. I saw that the possibilities for happiness are far-ranging and exhilarating.

I felt, finally, at home in this world.

2

The One True God

If God lived on earth, people would break his windows.

Jewish Proverb

Exercise your fancy and imagine that in the 1970s a child is a castaway on an uncharted, uninhabited island (no, not Gilligan's) at the tender age of five. All alone, she somehow manages to feed herself, stay alive and suffer no major injuries. She is very bright and has figured out lots of things about the world around her. She has developed her voice by imitating animal sounds, but has never, obviously, seen another human being. Then, when she is twenty years old, she is finally found by the U.S. Navy. She is introduced to the astonishing, frightening prospect of the real world. Being bright, she learns to speak and slowly she absorbs the almost unbelievably complex history of her kind — humans. She has wondered about so many things in her loneliness, and now, thanks to carefully chosen tutors, many of those questions are being answered. She studies her caretakers while they study her. They then decide to present religion to her in its many forms, allowing her to choose from among them.

This is the fanciful premise. Now try to imagine the task of presenting the world's religions to such a "clean slate" of a mind. The prospect is daunting. The entire concept of "god" is fraught with difficulties, not the least of which is defining the word "god." It cannot be done without resorting to a word like "supernatural," which has its own problems of definition. When viewed in this way, as a body of theological theories to be presented *en masse* to a fresh, unbiased mind, the glaring contradictions and inconsistencies of the world's religions are brought into sharp focus. In asking this fresh, unbiased mind (or any mind, for that matter) to believe in one of these theories, you will be forced, finally, to ask for the suspension of logic and reason. You will have to demand acceptance through "faith." It all boils down to faith. This is the fatally weak link in the chain.

Faith is the suspension of reason. Where reason prevails, faith has no place. Where faith prevails, reason cannot function. The two may not coexist. When people tell you to "open your heart and let God in," what they really mean is to stop using your brain and start sifting facts through the sieve of intuition and revelation rather than reason. This is an unacceptable means of understanding the world around us. In fact, a good general rule for the judging of *any* claim, about "god" or UFOs or pink elephants, would be to consider the extent to which you must suspend reason in order to believe it. The more you must suspend reason, the less likely the thing is to be true.

Revelation is the least likely source of reliable information. It is not subject to verification or falsification. And it has brought us such wonders as death at the stake for witchcraft, "visitors" from the planet Venus, and David Koresh in Waco, Texas. Pure reason would render such things unthinkable, since reason always defeats nonsense. Revelation and reason are fundamentally antagonistic.

Assuming you could clear this hurdle of presenting the concept of "god" without resorting to the suspension of reason (which probably can't be done) there are still many more problems. Which god or gods would you present to a thoroughly uninitiated newcomer? There are so many. There are thousands of different gods and goddesses who have been worshipped somewhere, sometime, by some people. Do you present them all? Do you, for example, present Re, the Egyptian Sun-God? Or do you just present the current "biggies"—Hinduism, Islam, Judaism, Christianity and Buddhism? In what order will you present them? How will you explain their drastic differences? How will you explain that God is always a male? And how will you answer the inevitable question —"But which religion is *right?*"

True Believers will inform you, of course, that their religion is the true religion. Arrogance is the only word for people who declare that only they possess the "eternal truths" while the vast majority of the world's population is wrong. There is not necessarily truth in numbers, but such lopsided percentages ought to give pause to any and all. Nevertheless, True Believers will swear, at great length and with much fervor if you don't stop them, that their truth is the only truth.

Consider Christianity. Although the *I'm right and the majority of the world is wrong* attitude is held by all major world religions, Christianity is the most familiar in America. Its basic tenet is that Jesus Christ is the Son of God and the Savior of humankind. If this is true, then the Jews and the Hindus and the Muslims are wrong. Buddhists, Confucianists and Taoists are wrong. The ancient Egyptians, the ancient Babylonians and ancient Aztecs were wrong. In fact, every human being who ever lived but did not accept Jesus Christ as Savior was or is wrong. This is going to prove to be an extremely large number of people, easily counted in the billions.

Christians are uncomfortable with these considerations, especially in discussing the ancients, who of course had no way of knowing about something that hadn't even happened yet. But these ticklish, vexing problems are tossed into the grab-bag of *The Lord Works In Mysterious Ways His Wonders To Perform,* which is supposed to satisfy the questioner. It does not satisfy.

According to Christianity's own doctrines, you either accept Christ as your Savior, thereby being "saved," or you reject Christ, thereby being "damned." This simplistic view fails to take into account the people who have never been exposed to Christian teachings, which is the vast majority of all the people who have ever lived. What about *their* souls? For example, what about Ramses II, ruler of Egypt, who lived over a thousand years before Christ? He lived his life, worshipped his Egyptian gods, and died without ever having heard of Jesus Christ. Will his soul go to Heaven or Hell? It wouldn't be fair if he automatically goes to Hell because he never had the chance to accept Christ even if he might have been so inclined. Such a cruel god, saying, in effect, "Well, you were born too soon — tough luck!" is thoroughly repellent and totally unacceptable.

However, if Ramses II automatically goes to Heaven without ever having had to clear the hurdle of accepting Christ, then that wouldn't be fair to all of the people who do indeed have to face the challenge of accepting or rejecting Christ, which includes the definite possibility of choosing wrong and being damned for all eternity. Why should Ramses II achieve eternal bliss without ever having to risk damnation? To my knowledge this problem has never been addressed satisfactorily except with vague comments about how God will work it out somehow, which is the same as saying, "I haven't the foggiest idea." So this problem is insolvable. But let us assume for the sake of argument that the problem doesn't even exist, which is what most Christians do anyway.

Now, if the Christians are correct in their beliefs, then everyone else is incorrect. It is not a question of worshipping the same god in different ways, as many religionists insist, trying desperately to unify all humankind into one religious brotherhood. Worldwide religious beliefs allow for no such unification, being as they are specific, unwavering and mutually exclusive. The god of Moses, assuming he is the One True God, either sent Jesus Christ as his son to be the savior of humankind or he didn't. If he did, anyone who worships a god who did not do this thing is not simply worshipping differently. He is worshipping a different god. If the one is right, then any others must be wrong.

Of course the same can be said about other religions. If, for example, the Prophet Muhammad was correct in his assertion that Jesus Christ was only another of God's prophets, no more and no less, then all of Christianity is wrong — not just different, but wrong. If Muhammad was also correct in the rest of his revelations as recorded in the Koran, then everyone who is not Muslim is *wrong*. Either Muhammad spoke eternal truths handed down from God or he did not. If he did, and you don't believe it, you are wrong.

Every major religion possesses this all-or-nothing quality wherein if it is correct then all others must be incorrect. There is real food for thought here. They cannot *all* be right, since they are thoroughly contradictory. Logic demands that no more than one of them may be correct. Those same laws of logic will of course allow for all of them to be incorrect, and a truly objective, unbiased observer, perhaps a clean slate of a mind, probably would consider this possibility the most likely. Nevertheless, for the purpose of argument let us take the position that Christianity is, after all, the one true religion. There are still problems.

Which form of Christianity is correct? T here are so many. In fact, would-be converters to Christianity should be getting together with all other Christians and working out one coherent, easy-to-present package that all Christians agree on. Only then should they try to peddle their wares, as it were, to nonbelievers. After all, if Christians can't agree with each other, why should a nonbeliever accept *any* Christian doctrines? What should be the criteria for choosing one over the others? The attractiveness of the church buildings? The music? The Bingo games?

Christians will naturally argue that things are not as chaotic as all that, pointing out that all Christians do worship, after all, the same god. This, however, is not true. Christians do not all worship the same god. God either speaks through the Pope in Rome or he does not. There is no room for a middle position here. He does or he does not. Which is it? A Roman Catholic worships a god who speaks through the Pope while a Baptist worships one who does not. They cannot be the same god.

No one, not even a god, can speak through the Pope and not speak through the Pope at the same time. If you argue that since God can do anything such a paradox *can* exist, then you must also grant that all of the other tenets of Christianity can also be said to exist and not exist at the same time, thereby contradicting the laws of logic and making Christianity an incomprehensible mish-mash of nonsense. Christ is the Son of God and he is not the Son of God. Humans have souls and they do not have souls. There is a Heaven and there is not a Heaven. Christ rose from the dead and he did not rise from the dead, and so on. No Christian anywhere will insist on suspending logic to this extent but this leaves us, then, with our still unanswered question. Does God speak through the Pope? Yes or no? If he does, then every single Christian except the Catholics is wrong for not believing this. If he does not, then every single Catholic is wrong.

There are many other equally divisive yes-or-no questions that can only be answered by declaring that some Christians, somewhere, are *wrong*. For example, did God speak to the prophet Joseph Smith, providing him with magic spectacles, that resulted in the Book of Mormon? Yes or no? If he did, then every single Christian except the Mormons is wrong for not believing this. If he did not, then every single Mormon is wrong.

Does God approve of prayer to saints? Yes or no? Is there such a place as purgatory? Yes or no? Is birth control a sin? Is there predestination? On and on, the questions serve to illuminate the striking differences between various Christian faiths, differences that cannot be easily dismissed. It is not true to say, as Christian apologists will insist, that these differences simply represent different ways of worshipping the same god. Different types of music, preferences in dress, choices regarding kneeling or standing, the use of candles and other such considerations definitely fall into this category representing styles of worship, and do not necessarily define a deity. But if you worship a god who considers birth control a sin and your neighbor worships a god who does not, then you are worshipping two different gods. It cannot be otherwise.

In The Beginning

In the pristine nothingness that existed before creation, God had options. Since the laws of nature had yet to be written by his own hand, there were no constraints of any kind as to what kind of universe he could create. God was free to do as he pleased. With this in mind it is difficult to understand why he then went on to create a world that produced earthquakes, volcanic eruptions, floods, hurricanes and tornadoes. These so-called natural disasters have killed and maimed millions upon millions of humans, not to mention other animals, as God very well knew they would even before he created them. Likewise, the organisms that cause polio, smallpox, tuberculosis, leprosy, syphilis, meningitis, measles, trichinosis, bubonic plague, and on and on, were all supposedly created by a loving god. But such a scenario strains credulity. Either these ghastly little microbes were not created by God, or God is not loving.

This line of reasoning can be carried forward, logically, to all aspects of creation. Why do animals eat each other? Because God created them that way — that's why. Why do volcanoes erupt? Because God created them that way. Why do people steal, rape and kill? Because God created them that way. Why did Adam and Eve sin? Because God created them that way. If you accept the idea of a world hand-crafted by an all-powerful deity, then all of these disasters and diseases befall us because God wants it that way. If he didn't want them to happen, they wouldn't. (Consider again the meaning of the word "omnipotent.") So the creationists are going to have to explain how it is that an all-merciful, loving god chose to create, for example, the polio virus. It defies rational explanation.

On the other hand, in an indifferent universe, without a reigning deity, where all life forms are equally important or unimportant, and where species evolve through natural selection, this perceived savagery in nature is very easy to explain. Survival is the name of the game, and if you can survive by eating some other creature or by becoming a parasite on some other creature, then so be it. This pressure for survival readily explains the restaurant-like quality found in nature, where big fish eat little fish, and giant fish eat big fish, and human beings eat all three. Less easy to understand is a god-created world where all the animals eat each other. Why would God arrange things like that, since his options were unlimited? Moreover, there is something very noxious about the thought of a supposedly loving god taking time somewhere during creation to bring about the existence of malaria.

Creationists want it both ways. Denying evolution, they insist that every single animal species was independently created by God, but then they go on to insist that God is not responsible for any harm caused by those very creations. This is nonsense. If God created the polio virus, then he is responsible for all polio victims. There is no complicated or sophisticated reasoning in this clear-cut, straightforward deduction.

Another attempt at shifting blame away from God involves blaming humans. Yes, the world is cruel. Yes, disasters and diseases have befallen us in unrelenting successions. However, none of this awful stuff existed, or so claim the creationists, until *after* the Fall (Adam's and Eve's first sin). The theory here is that *before* the Fall, there was no disease and there were no disasters. (Differences exist. Choose your Experts.) So Adam and Eve brought all this suffering on humankind by being disobedient in the Garden of Eden. The biggest problem with this theory, although there are many, is that it calls for a second creation. After the Fall, God would have had to create the whole realm of bacteria and viruses and fungi and parasites and venomous snakes and man-eating carnivores and so on. Then he would have had to rearrange the Earth's plate tectonics so as to allow for earthquakes and volcanic eruptions. The Earth's orbit would have to be altered in order to change the heat that drives global storm systems. And so on. In other words, a second creation would have had to take place. The first one is difficult enough to believe in, but this second one seems purely sadistic.

The more basic problem with this theory, which says in effect that you brought it all on yourselves, is that if God had wanted human beings who would not sin, he should have created human beings who would not sin. An all-powerful, all-knowing god cannot by definition be surprised or disappointed, since he would know full well everything that lay in the future. So his anger at Adam and Eve is unjustified and inexplicable since he already knew precisely what they were going to do. Nothing could have prevented this all-powerful god from creating perfect people, if that's what he wanted. Instead, though, he created a couple of losers and then turned around and cursed them, forever, for being losers. Talk about stacking the deck.

One of the most often cited arguments supporting the theory of creation involves the wonders of nature. Creationists will direct your attention to the beauty of a magenta sunset or the almost magical hovering of a hummingbird at a flower, and then triumphantly attack the notion that such wonders could "just happen." Such beauty must have a creator, they say.

But there is more to nature than sunsets and hummingbirds. What would those same ardent creationists say as they stood at the fringe of a recent volcanic eruption, watching the cooling lava flow that contained the charred bones of hundreds of its human victims? Would they claim that there must be a divine creator to explain this wonder of nature? Most likely they would not, but then they are being inconsistent.

The same god that created sunsets and hummingbirds also created leprosy, cystic fibrosis and Mt. Vesuvius. And it is impossible to believe that God supposedly cares one way or another if one tiny sparrow falls to the ground, as True Believers insist, since this same god is credited with creating the falcon, who will gobble up a half dozen sparrows for lunch. If this is a dog-eat-dog world, then the creationists can thank their loving god, who, according to their own beliefs, created all the suffering that has ever been.

Let Us Pray

Not only Christianity, but most religions, urge prayer. Prayer is a practice that cannot survive the harsh spotlight of logic. The three most often cited reasons for prayer are worship, confession and petition. (Differences exist. Choose your Experts.) The most popular form of prayer, petition, poses some complicated problems.

At first glance, asking God to do something or other seems perfectly logical. Who better to ask? But the only way that such asking makes sense is if there is a chance that you might receive a positive response. What would be the point of having billions of prayers offered beseechingly to a god who never intended at any time to answer a single one of them? A more pointless, time-wasting, soul-draining exercise is difficult to imagine, and a god who would demand such a practice would have to be sadistic. Such bait-and-switch tactics are difficult to attribute to *any* god, even the one who sent the Flood. On the other hand, if prayer is encouraged because there is a chance that requests will be granted, you run headlong into the unavoidable requirement to explain the seemingly capricious nature of some of these boons.

For example, a high-school student prays that he will pass a math exam even though he hasn't studied for it, and when he does pass he attributes this to God's intervention. Most religious leaders would agree with this. (Differences exist. Choose your Experts.) But if it is true, we are faced with a god who answers a single petition from a single person in the matter of a tenth-grade algebra test, but who chose to ignore the millions of prayers for liberation from concentration camps during World War II. There is a selection process at work here that is extremely difficult to grasp.

According to the "Lord's Prayer," people are supposed to ask, "Give us this day our daily bread." Why? If you ask, will it be done? If it won't be done, why should you ask? Since war and famine have brought death by starvation to many True Believers, this asking for daily bread seems pointless. If starvation happens to those who ask as well as to those who don't, then the explanation for starvation must lie in factors wholly unrelated to the asking. In other words, asking God for your daily bread has nothing to do with whether or not you will get it. So why are you supposed to ask for it?

Likewise, prayers of thanksgiving intrinsically impute to God complete control over your well-being. If you thank God for the food on your table, you are saying that he put it there. A necessary component of this premise, the other side of this coin, is that if there is *no* food on your table, God is responsible for that, too. The power to give necessarily includes the power to withhold. When you thank someone for a gift it is because you understand that he had the choice of not giving it to you, but chose to do so anyway. Thanking God for your food, then, is the same as saying "thank you" for not withholding food. You are offering thanks for not being allowed to starve.

Just as it would make no sense to thank your neighbors for a much needed rain shower, since they could not have played any role in producing the rain, so it would make no sense to thank God for the food on your table *unless* he definitely plays a role in getting that food to your table. And if he does, we are presented with the vexing question of just how he chooses to feed some while starving others. If the choice to put food on your table is God's, then the choice *not* to put food on someone else's table is also God's. So, then, why doesn't God feed all of us?

Starving babies are an awkward consideration on Thanksgiving Day, as we sit down to sumptuous turkey dinners, but if God puts the turkey on your table, he withholds it from countless others. Why? If God only feeds "his own," that would mean that the babies of those other than "his own" could starve without his caring, a heartless proposition. It would also mean that his own have never starved, which is certainly not true. Nor can it be said that all atheists starve. So how *does* God decide whom to feed? This question of God's priorities cannot be side-stepped if his participation in daily events is posited. If God has the power to feed all of us, but chooses not to, his reluctance must be explained in a way that is compatible with his purported omnipotence (all-powerfulness) and omnibenevolence (all-goodness). No one has yet managed to proffer such an explanation.

Trying to explain starvation by saying that God helps those who help themselves is a cruel, callous way to regard victims of crop failures from floods, drought or pestilence. And what about the babies? How can babies help themselves?

Likewise, trying to explain starvation by saying that we just can't understand the ways of God is a contradiction of all of the rest of Christian doctrine. Christians claim to know precisely how God wants his "children" to worship, how they should pray, how they should dress, what they should eat, how they should address their elders and so on, implying quite clearly that God's ways are indeed understood. But questions about the terrible reality of starved-to-death babies are met with vague shrugs as if such trivia did not need to be understood. But *someone* must accept responsibility for the haunting specter of starving children.

If food production and distribution on this Earth are solely the result of human activities, with no participation by God, then giving thanks to God for food is a misplaced, meaningless gesture. He has done nothing to deserve thanks, and we alone must answer for the cruel inequities. If, on the other hand, God does participate in the process, then thanks to him are due for our chocolate bars and imported cheeses, and he has a lot of starving babies to answer for.

All this talk of starvation is of course representative of and interchangeable with all human conditions. Whether you are considering illness, injury, or persecution, if you pray for deliverance from any of them, the results will be the same as with starvation — random and inexplicable.

So let's consider again prayers of supplication. Ending world hunger, a most admirable request, has yet to become a reality, in spite of countless prayers. So people are encouraged to pray, instead, for more easily achieved goals, like having Aunt Helen get over her cold soon, or for the kids to do well in school. Football players actually get on their knees and thank God for touchdowns. In a world that contains starvation, disease, murder and rape, such mundane considerations trivialize the role of a supposedly omnipotent god.

For every "miraculous" recovery by a seriously ill person that is attributed to God, there is a seriously ill person who is prayed for but dies anyway. Soldiers are prayed for and die, and soldiers are not prayed for but live. Bad things happen to good, prayed-for people, and bad things happen to bad people. Good things happen to good people and good things happen to bad people. In other words, the laws of probability are quite clearly in control here. All things are not made well for those who trust in God, and life can be very pleasant for those who do not. If judged only by the results that challenge the laws of probability, then the power of prayer is nil.

The One-Sided Triangle

For thousands of years Jews and Christians alike have been struggling desperately, though unsuccessfully, to convince the rest of the world that they were totally different from their primitive, pagan predecessors, who had gods for everything from toothaches to infertile goats. Jews and Christians have both claimed to be monotheistic — that is, to worship only one god. The Jews, at least, do only have their one Jehovah, but they were (some still are) waiting for the Messiah to come. Now, would this Messiah (savior) be a deity — a god — or not? Most probably he would not be just another Joe, come to Earth the way the rest of us do, completely mortal. However, if this Messiah *were* one-hundred percent mortal, then the Jews at least would have the right to a claim of monotheism.

The Christians, on the other hand, are in real trouble here. Explaining the Triune God (Father, Son and Holy Ghost) as a single entity requires extraordinary linguistic legerdemain. Jesus Christ, called the "Son of God" (the son of himself?) often prayed to God the Father (was he praying to himself?) and supposedly had the Holy Spirit descend upon him at his baptism by John the Baptist (did he descend upon himself?). As the early Christians tried frantically to distance themselves from their polytheistic, pagan contemporaries, this Father-Son-Holy Ghost business prompted the concept of the "Triune God," three personages in one, each different with different characteristics, but nevertheless only one "god." In other words, a one-sided triangle. The foolishness of this tortured reasoning is an insult to the most meager intelligence.

If you then throw in the myriad of "saints" to which the Catholics pray, the claim to monotheism actually becomes laughable. How many saints are prayed to? Has anyone really counted them all? Does anyone really know? How is praying to a saint to bring you children in any way different from earlier pagans who prayed to their goddesses for children? And the reverence, intent and supplication contained in the prayer that opens with "Our Father which art in Heaven" differ not in the slightest from the prayer that opens with "Hail Mary, full of grace."

Monotheism, as proclaimed today in Christianity, is an embarrassingly transparent sham.

The Old Rugged Cross

The Cross, that most powerful and pervasive symbol of Christianity, has been painted in oils, carved into woodwork and furniture, perched prominently on the tops of thousands of buildings, cried upon, prayed to, kissed fervently, worn as a necklace, embroidered into clothing and carved into mountainsides. Poems have been written about it, hymns have been sung about it, and people trace out its shape by touching forehead, chest and shoulders whenever the name of a dearly departed is even mentioned. This is some symbol.

A question immediately presents itself. Aren't Christians aware that the Cross was an instrument devised for human torture and death? How can such an ugly symbol ever be regarded as something holy and worthy of reverence? A crucifix symbolizes the worst thing we can possibly do to each other — inflict constant torture until death arrives. (If there is something worse we can do to one another, it's hard to imagine what it might be.) The entire concept is revolting and sickens even the less compassionate among us.

As Christians wax eloquent about salvation and eternally rapturous joy, it's easy to forget the actual physical events that supposedly made such rapture possible. The events consisted of a trial without jury, a scourging with a whip, a death by torture, followed by a three-day stay in a tomb for the deceased, during which time he somehow descended into Hell, followed by the supposed resurrection of the dead body. There's a lot of terrible stuff going on in this incredible scenario.

(It should be noted that there were many pre-Christian savior-gods who were born of virgins, died for the sins of humankind, rose from the dead, and ascended into Heaven, making it highly unlikely that the Jesus story is true.)

But even if Christians were correct in their assertions that Jesus truly walked this Earth as a human being, and then truly died as they say he did, this story demands a close scrutiny of "The Old Rugged Cross."

First there is the unavoidable problem of explaining just why the all-merciful God of Creation felt the need to ask for a human sacrifice in the first place. I've dealt with this topic elsewhere, but it always bears repeating. We know from history that the practice of sacrificing to the gods is an ancient and primitive one. Early humans sacrificed animals, plants and each other, in the sensible-to-them attempt to placate the blood-thirsty gods they believed were controlling their lives.

We have the horrific example of the Aztecs who ripped the hearts out of living human victims, as blood splattered everywhere, and deities were presumed to be placated by such carnage. (Hopefully you're not eating lunch while you're reading this.) Modern Christians look at such primitive sacrifices with condescension and disdain, failing to recognize the darkly humorous irony of their position. At the very heart of their own religion is a bloody death-by-torture. I'm not sure which is worse — having your heart cut out or being nailed to a tree until you die. I'd say it's too close to call.

But Christian disdain for the Aztecs is a classic example of the pot calling the kettle black. Death is death. Torture is torture. Pain is pain. Trying to present such barbaric practices as having some glorious higher purpose does not change the original act of human blood-letting. Assigning to God the blame for the barbarism does not help the Christians' case. It simply renders their own god barbaric.

The idea of one god-like human taking the rap, so to speak, for all of humanity's evil-doings, by dying somehow, is not only incomprehensible and illogical, but contradicts the Christian concept of Heaven and Hell. If humankind's sins were all washed away with Jesus' death, how can Hell await anyone? If Hell awaits, what was the point of Jesus' sacrificial death? And again, it must be explained why a loving God would want anyone to suffer, die *or* go to Hell. This theological tangle has to be left to molder on its own. Logical minds can never unravel it.

So, getting back to the Cross, please try a mental exercise. Clear your mind of all preconceived images of crosses and crucifixes. Forget the majestic crosses towering over huge cathedrals. Forget the stained glass windows. Forget the 24-karat-gold necklaces with diamond-studded crosses. Forget the beautifully crafted crosses inlaid with ivory and jade. Forget the Vatican's priceless art collection. Wipe it all from your mind and picture, instead, two roughly-hewn, small-to-medium sized tree trunks or branches. Now picture someone nailing these two pieces of wood together to form a crude cross. Assume it's a slave working under the direction of a Roman soldier.

(Purportedly the condemned prisoners were forced to carry their own crosses to their places of death. You can't help but wonder what would have happened if they had simply refused. What sort of threats could conceivably have been used to force those unfortunate individuals to carry their own crosses? Could things possibly have been made worse for them? "You'd better pick up those crosses, you guys, or you're in *big* trouble." Well, it's just a thought.)

Now, imagine someone, slave or soldier, physically nailing a human being onto this cross. He would have to drive nails through the hands and feet of the condemned prisoner, causing, one may assume, a great deal of pain accompanied by a great deal of screaming. Blood would either run or spurt, perhaps staining the person doing the nailing. (Let's *definitely* hope you're not eating your lunch now.) Some sort of ropes or cloths would undoubtedly be used to tie the victim's arms to the cross, since the writhing body might otherwise rip the nails straight through the hands, causing the sufferer to fall off of the cross. And this wouldn't do.

Next, with the help of able-bodied individuals, the cross, with its screaming attachment, will be hoisted into the air, its base firmly planted in the ground, so that cross and condemned can either bake in the sun or be drenched with rain, depending on the weather. Then, the victim will hang for days, in anguished torment, until he dies. That's all there is to it. This is your basic crucifixion.

If a soldier were to feel some sympathy for a victim or just got tired of listening to the screams, he might take his sword and dispatch the victim early, hastening death and ending the noise. But other than that, it's really just a matter of agonized suffering until you die.

This nauseating scenario is presented, unbelievably, as proof of God's boundless mercy. Murder your own son, gruesomely, and then inform mortals that now their sins have all been washed away with Jesus' copiously-spilled blood. However, everyone still runs the risk of going to Hell if they cheat on their income taxes. What is wrong with this picture?

If this has been terribly offensive, it was not intended to be. This story of the crucifixion belongs to the Christians, not the author. But only by recognizing the Cross for what it really was, an obscene instrument of torture and death, can anyone properly evaluate the religion known as Christianity. There is not now, nor was there ever, anything wondrous, rapturous or beautiful about that horrifying instrument of torture known as The Old Rugged Cross.

Those Good Old Family Values

A few years ago all of America was subjected to the bizarre spectacle of the Vice President of the United States, Dan Quayle, attacking TV's Murphy Brown for glorifying unmarried parenthood and for mocking traditional "Family Values." (How *do* you spell potato[e], anyway?) Ever since, the rallying cry of the Religious Right has been Family Values, which they claim come from the Bible. But what exactly are traditional Family Values? Show me two different families and I'll show you two different sets of Family Values.

However, the Religious Right has decided that Family Values are synonymous with *Christian* Family Values. We, as citizens in a democracy, are being urged by our government leaders to adopt a certain religious viewpoint. That in itself is repugnant and unconstitutional. But it is also a bit of a paradox, because there are so few Family Values even mentioned in the

Christian Bible, and those mentioned are vague at best.

The Old Testament is filled with references to Patriarchs and their many wives and concubines. King Solomon had seven hundred wives and three hundred concubines. Concubines were simply status symbols (the more money you had, the more concubines you could afford) intended to provide their male owners with a titillating array of sexual partners to choose from. It was like owning your own whorehouse. Now *there* is a solid Family Value. What could be more wholesome than for a man to be able to have sex with three different women every night for a solid year without ever having to repeat?

All of the children of all of those concubines were considered bastards, unlike all of the children of all of those wives. So while Solomon obviously had a good time, is the Religious Right asking us to believe that all of those children, resulting from all of that multi-partner sexual intercourse, grew up in the warm, secure atmosphere of traditional Family Values?

(For ease of reading, all biblical sources are listed at the end of this section.)

Also in the Old Testament are the so-called Ten Commandments, one of which instructs men not to covet another man's property, and a wife is described as part of that property. Girls found not to be virgins on their wedding night were to be stoned to death. If the people didn't obey God properly, he would force them to eat their own children. Female slaves could be used sexually. Homosexuals, who were obviously part of someone's family, were to be put to death simply because they were homosexuals. The elderly King David had a young virgin brought to his bed to "warm" him up. If your son was a drunkard, he was to be killed. Virgins were nonchalantly listed as "booty" in war. As discipline, children were to be beaten with rods. Family Values?

The only value worth mentioning in the Ten Commandments is the directive for children to honor their parents (rod-beatings notwithstanding, apparently). But in that same list of directives, nowhere are parents directed to love and respect their children, and surely that is equally, if not more, important in any family setting.

These Old Testament practices could not possibly be further removed from any sort of ideal Family Values. Not only is there no disapproval shown for these terrible practices, but they were actually ordered, by God, to be engaged in. The out-of-context argument that is always raised when these biblical examples are proffered, will not stand. There *is* no healthy, family-oriented context into which the above obscenities may be inserted.

The Christian Religious Right may not distance itself from these Old Testament obscenities, since the New Testament is based upon, and inseparable from, the Old Testament. And in any event, the New Testament scarcely fares any better than the Old. First of all, there is the obvious fact that Jesus never married or had any children, so the Great Teacher of Family Values never loved a woman or knew what it meant to stay up all night with his colicky baby and still feel love for the child.

Nor did Jesus show any love toward his own mother. When she asked him a favor, he replied, "Woman, what have I to do with you?" Why would he embarrass his mother like that? What must she have felt? He refused to bless his mother. He never expressed any thanks whatsoever to Joseph, his stepfather, whose labors, one may rightly assume, put the food in Jesus' mouth from infancy to adulthood. Jesus actually disowned his own mother and referred, instead, to his disciples as being his "mother and brothers." When a disciple requested a temporary leave to go home to bury his father, Jesus said no. Surely burying your loved ones, showing respect for your dead, should rank quite high in any group of Family Values. Apparently Jesus disagreed. He also demanded that any who wanted to be his disciples must *hate* their own father, mother, wife and children. He stated that all who had abandoned homes, parents, children and families to follow him would "receive a hundred times as much and inherit eternal life." (Abandon your children?) He asserted that all his disciples belonged "to one family," relegating family units, as we know them, to oblivion.

Jesus nonchalantly told a parable about ten virgins who were preparing to marry the same man on the same night, as if such sexual arrangements were perfectly normal and moral. While it may have been a common practice, since the Old Testament smiles on polygamy, shouldn't Jesus have found such an offensive scenario unfit for one of his lesson stories? It's like trying to help your child in arithmetic by saying, "Let's say Daddy is a pimp and he runs a string of six girls. If two of his girls leave him, but then one more joins him, how many hookers will Daddy have working the streets altogether?" Both female-degrading scenarios are disgusting and equally inappropriate for lesson-teaching.

The New Testament tells us that we have a better chance to get to Heaven if we *don't* marry, and that, just as in the Old Testament, all homosexuals must be put to death. We are told that it is good for a man not to touch a woman, that effeminate men cannot go to Heaven, and that women should keep their silence and learn only from their husbands. We learn that wives should "submit" themselves to their husbands, and that women should talk to their husbands in "fear." Family Values?

Probably the most offensive family reference in the entire New Testament is St. Paul's denigration of marriage. Paul, who almost single-handedly brought the religion known as Christianity into being, was a self-proclaimed celibate. He flatly stated that he wished everyone could be asexual like he was. (If his wish had come true, human history would have come to a screeching halt as extinction embraced humankind.) He said, "I say therefore to the unmarried and widows, It is good for them if they abide even as I. But if they cannot contain, let them marry: for it is better to marry than to burn." So then, according to the most influential writer in the New Testament, marriage is an undesirable thing, something to be avoided unless you're just so horny you can't stand it. Could marriage be presented in a more demeaning way? Murphy Brown differed from Paul in her view of marriage. Unlike Paul, Brown did not believe you should get married just because you're horny. Many would agree with her.

Even Jesus himself says that those who will be accounted worthy to obtain life after death (resurrection) shall not be married. Period. Hard to get a family going that way, with or without any Family Values. But Jesus' words are quite clear: those of us who choose to marry cannot achieve Heaven. Do you suppose the leaders of the so-called Moral Majority are aware of this? And do you suppose that family life could be debased more than by Jesus' own scathing words about marriage? Jesus' plan, like Paul's, would eliminate families altogether, and thereby end the entire human race. It is The-End-Of-The-World-Is-At-Hand stuff.

Once again, any "context" argument fails here. The above offensive references simply don't belong anywhere in a Bible purported to be the standard of excellence in Family Values. Actually, they don't belong anywhere at all.

The self-appointed leader of the Religious Right, the Catholic Church, forbids all of its clergy to marry and have families. Just how does that support Family Values? Supposedly the clergy can simply ignore their sexual urges just because they take a vow. Then, these unmarried nonparents are supposed to counsel parishioners on Family Values. This seems to be the height of foolishness.

Before any more fundamentalists point to their Christian Bible and preach about values, they should read that Bible, and they should read *all* of it. After doing so, they will realize that their claim to the moral high ground holds no merit whatsoever, and is an embarrassment to all concerned.

Sources:

King Solomon's wives. (1 Kings 11:3)
A wife is property. (Exodus 20:17)
Non-virginal brides must be murdered. (Deuteronomy 22:20,21)
Eat your own children. (Leviticus 26:29) and (Deuteronomy 28:53)
Female slaves can be used sexually. (Exodus 21:7–11)
Homosexuals should die.(Leviticus 20:13) and (Romans 1:26–32)
Old King David's virgin "warm-up." (1 Kings 1:1–3)
Stubborn, rebellious, drunkard sons must be murdered. (Deuteronomy 21:18–21)
Wartime booty, virgins, are to be saved and raped. (Numbers 31:17,18)

Beat children with rods. (Proverbs 23:13,14)
Honor parents. (Exodus 20:12)
Jesus rebukes his mother. (John 2:3,4)
Jesus refuses to bless his mother. (Luke 11:27,28)
Jesus disowns mother, prefers disciples. (Matthew 12:48–50)
Jesus disallows a disciple to bury his father. (Matthew 8:21,22)
Jesus says you must hate your whole family. (Luke 14:26)
Jesus orders disciples to abandon families. (Matthew 19:29)
Jesus' parable of the ten virgins. (Matthew 25:1–13)
Jesus says Heaven is only for unmarried. (Luke 20:34,35)
Paul says men should not touch women.(1 Corinthians 7:1)
Effeminate men may not go to Heaven.(1 Corinthians 6:9)
Women keep silent, learn only from husbands. (1 Corinthians 14:34,35)
Women must submit to husbands. (1 Timothy 2:11,12)
Women must speak to husbands in fear. (1 Peter 3:1–7)
Paul praises an asexual lifestyle. (1 Corinthians 7:7,8)
Paul says marry only if you're uncontrollably horny. (1 Corinthians 7:9)

But He That Believeth Not . . . .

There is a strong tendency in this country to brand nonbelievers as Communists or anarchists or criminals or pornographers or dope-peddlers or some sleazy combination thereof. Atheists are considered to be the scum of the Earth. For too long, the word "atheist" has been so badly maligned as to have lost its original meaning. It is a simple word with a simple meaning. But thanks to the efforts of religious zealots, that simple meaning has been corrupted to the point where even nonbelievers shy away from it, thinking it means a whole lot more than it does. It has become the Granddaddy of all buzzwords.

Most of us, even some nonbelievers, have quietly accepted the transforming of that little seven-letter word into a four-letter word. It has become an epithet. Religionists have put their own (sick) spin on a perfectly innocent word, and it should not be allowed to stand.

Even in some freethought circles that simple little word "atheist" is studiously avoided, as people scramble around in a desperate search for euphemisms. Most people believe that the term "agnostic" is a neutral, fence-sitting, middle position. But it's not. There are only two kinds of people — those who believe in a god and those who don't. (And, yes, all babies are atheists.) Agnostics feel that they can stand on the sidelines while theists and atheists slug it out. But what they fail to realize is that while they are standing on those sidelines, they, too, either believe in a god or they do not.

Any person who does not believe in a god, whether by denying that one exists, or by saying "god" can't be understood, is an atheist — a person without theistic belief. Undecided or indifferent, an agnostic does not believe in a god. If he did, he'd be a theist. Therefore, an agnostic is an atheist.

When Thomas Huxley coined the word "agnostic" in 1869, he may have intended it as a bit of a joke. He lamented the fact that his peers were all some sort of *"-ists"* (deists, atheists, pantheists) while all he could say about himself was that he *didn't know* the answers to the questions of existence, and, therefore, didn't know what to call himself. So he made up the word "agnostic." It stems from the Greek root *gnosis* ("to know") so agnosticism means, literally, "not to know." Huxley most likely was having a bit of fun in calling himself an "I-can't-know-*ist*." Nevertheless, people eagerly embrace the term "agnostic," thinking it's neutral, but as we've seen, it is not. You still must commit.

Christians have pounded away at the word "atheism" incessantly. George Bush was reported to have said that atheists should not even be considered citizens. But the word has absolutely nothing whatsoever to do with politics, morality, behavior, goodness, badness, cowardice or personality traits. It simply signifies the absence of a belief in a deity. That's it. There's no more. Not even *Webster's* can say any more about it. You can be a god-less conservative or a god-less liberal; a god-less nudist, or a god-less prude; a god-less murderer or a god-less philanthropist.

Someone once referred to himself as a "fanatical agnostic." The term has a nice ring to it, but what is it really saying? It is saying that he is positively fanatic in his inability to know something. Does that make sense?

The word "agnostic" really should be used as an adjective, not a noun. If you acknowledge a specific deity, you are a plain old theist. If you believe that, yes, there is a god out there but we simply can't comprehend the nature of that god, then you are an *agnostic theist*. You are acknowledging an *unknowable* deity. If you don't know whether there's a god out there or not, but you don't acknowledge one, you are an *agnostic atheist*. You are not acknowledging a deity. If you believe that there is no god out there, and you also don't think there could be, you are just a plain old atheist.

So, if you consider yourself an agnostic, ask yourself this question: Do you acknowledge a deity? Think about it for a moment. The question is not whether or not you think a deity *might* exist, somehow, somewhere. The question is whether or not, at this moment, you, personally, acknowledge one. Do you?

Logically, you can only answer yes or no.

But we don't like to be called atheists. When we hear the word "atheist" spoken, we also tend to hear, subconsciously, the slanderous adjectives that have been heaped on it by religionists. Though only "atheist" is *spoken*, what we *hear* is "left-wing, Commie, pinko, subversive, scum-bag atheist." (The word "nontheist" carries no such baggage, which, since it's a precise synonym, says a great deal.) But no matter which words we use — freethinker, atheist, nonbeliever, or whatever — society will not tolerate the lack of belief. It will respect almost all religious beliefs, *even though they positively contradict each other,* but atheism is unacceptable. Why is this?

Priests rape little boys, television evangelists patronize prostitutes and steal from poverty-stricken shut-ins, and Muslims and Christians even today murder each other in "holy" wars. If you look backward in history the number of terrible crimes committed in the name of religion is appalling. Yet all of this despicable behavior is readily forgiven, "in the name of God," even though most of it was *done* in the name of God. But a law-abiding, kind, generous person, who happens also to be an atheist, will be shunned openly, and not long ago would have been run out of town on a rail. What is so threatening about a nonbeliever?

Catholics and Protestants can live side by side, worship their differing deities side by side, and make no attempt at changing each other's beliefs, even though those beliefs are mutually exclusive, meaning *someone's* wrong. Then, they will both send out missionaries into the darkest recesses of Borneo, trying to convert the natives to their own "true" religion. This is ridiculous.

It means that whether or not these beliefs are right or wrong is less important than simply increasing your head count. But this will of course have the effect of lessening the head count of the real enemy — nonbelievers.

If True Believers were serene and certain in their beliefs, they would feel the need to convert not only nonbelievers but *different* believers as well. Christians claim, for example, that the only reason they send out missionaries is to share the joy of the knowledge of eternal salvation through Jesus Christ. If that's true, then they should be standing out in front of every synagogue, mosque and Buddhist temple in this country and preaching their joyous news to these folks. They should stick with it until they have converted everyone, and only then should they head out for Borneo.

There is a tremendous number of "closet" atheists. Because of the stigma wrongly attached to that group, many atheists are content with, and sometimes coerced into, keeping their lack of belief to themselves. Many atheists try not to challenge the cherished beliefs of people they care about, although they could easily do so, because they would derive no pleasure out of possibly stripping loved ones of any of those comforting, cherished beliefs.

This same courteous consideration is very rarely seen, however, when believers approach nonbelievers. Not only do so many believers want to cram their own beliefs down your throat, but their fanaticism in attempting it is almost frightening. A couple of hundred years ago, it was more than frightening. It was lethal. If you didn't believe the right stuff you were burned at the stake in the Roman Catholic Church's "Holy" Inquisition. We seem to have passed through that phase, hopefully forever (even though in Islam "holy" wars continue unabated) but the intense desire to bring nonbelievers into the fold is still very visible. Yet this is putting the cart in front of the horse.

As mentioned elsewhere, the most logical approach to the problem of Belief would be for the leaders of all the world's religions to get together and hammer out some sort of worldwide agreement, and then go out and present it to the rest of the world. The reason this will never happen is that a head-on collision between the world's major religions would demonstrate clearly that the groups are irreconcilable. No agreement could ever be reached unless the majority of the world's believers abandoned entirely their own beliefs and then adopted a totally alien set of beliefs. Not only could this never happen, but even if it could happen, it would cast real doubts on the newly-elected world religion — the winner, as it were. For if all the other religions could be dismissed as being "wrong," what guarantees are there that the remaining one is right?

So worldwide unanimity based on today's religions can never exist. And although each religion secretly believes all the others are wrong, they nevertheless bolster each other by agreeing that some sort of belief system is needed. This is why the atheist's position is so very annoying. You're *all* wrong, says the atheist; gods and demons and paradise and damnation are myth and folklore, and nothing more. This bald assertion is too jolting, too harsh. And given the wildly divergent natures of various religions, the disquieting possibility that they *are* all wrong is something better left unexamined. For intelligent religionists, dealing straight on with intelligent atheists causes them to feel like they are looking at themselves in the mirror after partying all night. They'd rather not do it, and they're not going to like what they see.

Life can be beautiful, profound and awe-inspiring, even without an irate god threatening you with eternal torment. The charge that atheists cheapen life in that they don't hold it dearly enough because they don't believe in a higher being has it backwards. Rather, the believer in an afterlife is the one who holds life too cheaply, looking at life on this Earth as little more than a temporary, unimportant kind of prelude to the real life — that after death. How could you possibly cheapen life more than by making such a claim?

Nor is there anything uplifting or life-valuing about the assertion that all of humankind, including the sweetest newborn baby, is worthy only of divine contempt and suitable only for eternal agony. The only way to avoid this deserved fate, so they say, is to grovel before the god who created us and apologize profusely for being exactly the way he created us. Then, we should give thanks for the fact that someone a long time ago was gruesomely nailed to a piece of wood and allowed to die of this torture, as a bloody atonement to placate the god who created this whole mess to begin with. Aside from being confusing and barbaric, this assessment of humanity places our intrinsic value as somewhat more than blue-green algae and somewhat less than a boll weevil.

In addition, if we fail to have water sprinkled on our heads while the right words are being spoken, and/or if we fail to say the right words ourselves at certain special times, and/or if we fail to perform certain rituals, then we will still go to eternal agony, even if we never do an unkind thing in our whole lives. We are nevertheless supposed to be prostrate with gratitude because God may, possibly, refrain from torturing us for all eternity. This refraining, when it happens, is referred to as "the grace of God." Many people would challenge the use of the word "grace," and would feel no desire whatever to say thank you.

This may be an unsympathetic summary of the Christian overview of life on Earth, but it is nevertheless accurate. A more demeaning view of human life may be possible, though maybe not. It certainly can't be considered uplifting. A nonbeliever feels that since this life is all there is, we should treasure and enjoy it. A believer feels that we should spend this lifetime flogging ourselves for being unworthy, wicked, evil and sinful. Which view embodies the greater reverence for life?

3

The Good Book

Immorality, perversion, infidelity, cannibalism, etc., are unassailable by church and civic league if you dress them up in the togas and tallhiths of the Good Book.

Ben Hecht, *A Child of the Century*

When Christian leaders urge you to read the Bible, they don't really mean it. What they mean is that you should read certain chapters and certain verses. They will even interpret them for you, translating them into everyday life. As you listen to Christian teachers, you will immediately be aware that certain chapters and verses are repeatedly quoted and analyzed while others are totally ignored. Why should this be? If it is all the word of God, isn't it all equally valid and equally valuable?

Very few people, including the clergy, have read the entire

Bible, and most Christians have read only prized snippets. But only those who have read the entire book, *including the clergy*, have any right at all to say anything about it. This standard is applied to all other books, so why not the Bible? Anyone who even begins to offer a critique on a book he has not read will be hooted down and told to do his homework before opening his mouth. The same should apply to the Bible. Any Christian who has not read the entire Bible, Genesis through Revelation, has no right to say anything about the book. Period.

A thorough reading of the Bible would probably shock most Christians. There's a lot of stuff in that book that is silly, or terribly offensive, or just plain disgusting, or all three. Some of the stories in the Bible are violent enough to hold their own with a Rambo movie. For example:

"Wherefore David arose and went, he and his men, and slew of the Philistines two hundred men; and David brought their foreskins, and they gave them in full tale to the king, that he might be the king's son in law. And Saul gave him Michal his daughter to wife." (1 Samuel 18:27)

"And it came to pass, when the letter came to them, that they took the king's sons, and slew seventy persons, and put their heads in baskets, and sent him them to Jezreel.

"And there came a messenger, and told him, saying, They have brought the heads of the king's sons. And he said, Lay ye them in two heaps at the entering in of the gate until the morning." (2 Kings 10:7,8)

❖ ❖ ❖

"And there was a great famine in Samaria . . . ."

"And the king said unto her, What aileth thee? And she answered, This woman said unto me, Give thy son, that we may eat him to day, and we will eat my son to morrow.

"So we boiled my son, and did eat him: and I said unto her on the next day, Give thy son, that we may eat him: and she hath hid her son." (2 Kings 6:25,28,29)

There is no justification consistent with moral, civilized behavior, for the relating of such atrocities, let alone the performing of them. Sexual mutilation of dead bodies? Baskets full of heads? Cannibalism? Why are these gruesome stories in a book about a supposedly all-merciful god? Can you imagine reading these stories to your young children? If that doesn't send them screaming into the night, it's hard to imagine what will. Children of course love to be scared by Fairy Tales and ghost stories, but they know that these are just that — tales. The Bible, however, is presented as the absolute truth, every single word of it, foreskins and all. What a chilling thought.

Thou Shalt Not Kill

The often cited commandment against killing, "Thou shalt not kill," is so riddled with exceptions as to be almost a macabre comedy. The Old Testament, which contains the so-called Ten Commandments, contains little else but killing, all heartily approved of by God. The following list includes some, but by no means all, of the people chosen to be murdered by God in the Old Testament:

Judith Hayes' List of Murders
Committed by the God of the Bible

1. The entire population of the earth at the time of Noah, except for eight survivors. (Genesis 7:23)
2. Everyone in Sodom and Gomorrah. (Genesis 19:24,25)
3. Amalek and his people. (Exodus 17:8–16)
4. 3,000 Israelites. (Exodus 32:27,28)
5. 14,700 Jews. (Numbers 16:44–49)
6. The people of Og. "So they smote him, and his sons, and all his people, until there was none left him alive: and they possessed his land." (Numbers 21:33–35)
7. 24,000 people. (Numbers 25:4–9)
8. All Midianite males. (Numbers 31:6–12)
9. The Ammonites. (Deuteronomy 2:19–21)
10. The Horims. (Deuteronomy 2:22)
11. The Amorites. ". . . utterly destroyed the men and the women and the little ones." (Deuteronomy 2:33–35)
12. The Hittites, Girgashites, Amorites, Canaanites, Perizzites, Hivites, and Jebusites. ". . . thou shalt smite them, and utterly destroy them;" (Deuteronomy 7:1–5)
13. Everyone in Jericho but one family. (Joshua 6:20–25)
14. 12,000 people of Ai. (Joshua 8:19–29)
15. All the people of Makkedah. (Joshua 10:28)
16. All the people of Libnah. (Joshua 10:29,30)
17. All the people of Gezer. (Joshua 10:33)
18. All the people of Eglon. (Joshua 10:34,35)
19. All the people of Hebron. (Joshua 10:36,37)
20. All the inhabitants of the land of Goshen. ". . . until they had destroyed them, neither left they any to breathe." (Joshua 11:12–16)

21 10,000 Perizzites and Canaanites. (Judges 1:4)
22 The inhabitants of Hormah, Gaza, Askelon, Ekron. (Judges 1:17–19)
23 10,000 Moabites. (Judges 3:29)
24 600 Philistines. (Judges 3:31)
25 All the hosts of Sisera. (Judges 4:16)
26 120,000 Midianites. (Judges 8:10)
27 1,000 Philistines. (Judges 15:15)
28 25,100 Benjaminites. (Judges 20:35)
29 50,070 people of Bethshemesh. (1 Samuel 6:19)
30 All the Amalekites. "Slay both man and woman, infant and suckling . . . ." (1 Samuel 15:3–7)
31 200 Philistine men, to obtain their foreskins, in order to buy a bride. (1 Samuel 18:27)
32 22,000 Syrians. (2 Samuel 8:5)
33 40,000+ Syrians. (2 Samuel 10:18)
34 The Ammonites of Rabbah, tortured to death by the great King David. (2 Samuel 12:29–31)
35 70,000 people. (2 Samuel 24:15)
36 Every man in Edom. (1 Kings 11:15)
37 All the prophets of Baal. (1 Kings 18:40)
38 127,000 Syrians. (1 Kings 20:28–30)
39 Moabite captains & "fifties." (2 Kings 1:9–14)
40 42 children, eaten by bears. (2 Kings 2:23,24)
41 185,000 Assyrians killed in their sleep. (2 Kings 19:35)
42 500,000 men of Israel. (2 Chronicles 13:16–20)
43 20,000 Edomites. (2 Chronicles 25:11,12)
44 120,000 Judeans in one day. (2 Chronicles 28:5,6)
45 75,500+ people. (Esther 9:12–14)

Today any one of these episodes would cause worldwide outrage.

As you read on you find that God expressly demands, in this Holy Bible, the *death* of witches, homosexuals, idolaters, adulterers, anyone who curses their parents, anyone doing work on the Sabbath, anyone having sex with the wrong in-laws, any girl not found to be virginal on her wedding night, and anyone who lets a dangerous ox roam about freely. This goes on and on and on until you finally throw the "Good" book down and become convinced that God most assuredly enjoys killing people more than any other activity, since that is the most common activity described in the blood-drenched pages of the Old Testament.

You are also faced with biblical passages such as these:

". . . their infants shall be dashed in pieces, and their women with child shall be ripped up." (Hosea 13:16)

"Their children also shall be dashed to pieces before their eyes; their houses shall be spoiled and their wives ravished." (Isaiah 13:16)

". . . and they shall have no pity on the fruit of the womb; their eye shall not spare children." (Isaiah 13:18)

"Then Menahem smote Tiphsah, and all that were therein, and the coasts thereof from Tirzah: because they opened not to him, therefore he smote it; and all the women therein that were with child he ripped up." (2 Kings 15:16)

❖ ❖ ❖

It is not possible to read these Charles Manson-like passages and at the same time claim that the Bible teaches only reverence for life. Less reverence cannot be fathomed. Any compassionate human being cannot read these horrible descriptions of murder without having the stomach turn. And no amount of rationalizing can justify any of it. Such descriptions render the Bible obscene.

Christian apologists will explain, earnestly and patiently, that killing and murdering are not the same thing. The ancient Hebrew words for "murder" and "kill" are different, you see. And there were translation errors made throughout the Old Testament, and especially in the Ten Commandments, you see. That means that the commandment should read, "Thou shalt not murder" rather than "Thou shalt not kill," you see. So when God ordered entire communities to be slaughtered, including the babies, he was ordering only that they be killed, not murdered. You see.

This sort of linguistic hairsplitting is intelligence-insulting, and betrays an astonishing callousness. Dead babies are dead babies, and I don't care *which* Hebrew verb you use to describe how they got that way. The obscenity of the destruction of Samaria, as described in Hosea 13:16, cannot be translated out of trouble. The verse, in its entirety, states, "Samaria shall become desolate; for she hath rebelled against her God: they shall fall by the sword: their infants shall be dashed in pieces, and their women with child shall be ripped up."

Well, that paints a pretty clear picture. You can play Name That Verb forever, but you will never change the monstrous nature of that appalling directive.

Since most of us have never dashed an infant to pieces, it is a challenge even to imagine how one might go about doing it. Try to envision such a thing, and as you do so, freeze your face muscles and go look in a mirror. You will see pain, shock, disgust, and perhaps a bit of nausea. But try not to sidestep this mental exercise. We are talking about the "Holy" Bible here, so let's plow through this.

Imagine, then, grabbing, say, a six-week-old, screaming infant away from its equally screaming mother. How would you "dash" the tiny baby to pieces? Perhaps you would grab the baby by its ankles and then swing it, like a golf club, smashing its little head against a stone wall or a tree, until its skull cracked and its brains spilled out. That should certainly qualify as dashing in pieces.

As for "ripping up" the pregnant women, it would probably just be a matter of using a sword and stabbing at their swollen bellies, repeatedly, until the fetuses were destroyed and the women were, literally, ripped up and lying, dead, in pools of their own blood.

(At this point, you might want to make note, again, of your facial expression.)

As for the rest, all of the children, teenagers, men and non-pregnant women, they would most likely just be killed in the normal way. Stab and slash at them until they die. And then, when you were all done, and you had carried out God's orders, you would be looking at a scene of bloody devastation. There would be dead bodies and body parts strewn across several acres of land, assuming anyone tried to run away, a fairly safe assumption. They would probably not have lined up in inspection formation, waiting to be slaughtered.

The killers (not murderers, mind you) would themselves be splattered with blood and tissue, and they'd have to step through pieces of brain, and fetal parts, and various organs and so on, to reassemble with their cohorts. There would undoubtedly be cheers all around, for a successful mission and a job well done. No doubt about it. Samaria had become desolate.

Whether or not the killers would bury the corpses would depend, presumably, on whether or not they planned to stay and occupy the land. If so, burials would be called for or else they wouldn't be able to stand the stench. If not, they would most likely just leave the corpses to rot.

In either event, God's will would have been done.

This has not been an exercise in gratuitous violence. The lurid descriptions were necessary to make a very important point. In response to my column in *Freethought Today* (the newspaper published by the Foundation that published this book) Christians have taken me to task, and repeatedly, harshly and condescendingly criticized me for using the word "murder" instead of "kill" to describe events such as the above. Christian fundamentalists take the incredible position that there is somehow a difference; that God did not order any babies to be murdered, but only killed. Smugly, they point this out to me, as if they had achieved some higher moral ground. My mind boggles at that concept. For if the above obscenities are not descriptions of murder, then murder does not exist.

It must be remembered that the above massacre was ordered because the people of Samaria had rebelled against God. But how can a baby rebel against God? Have you ever seen such a thing? How could you tell if it happened? Once again, though, biblical apologists have the answer. You see, the babies would have grown up to be wicked, godless sinners if allowed to live. So they had to die, you see. But the problem with this explanation is that those babies had only one destiny — to become dead babies. You see?

In any event, the slaughter was ordered because the people were not worshipping correctly. But isn't that exactly why Hitler went after the Jews? Is there a difference between the two atrocities? Were God's dead babies okay, while Hitler's dead babies were wrong? Shall we sit down and try to figure out which Hebrew verb, "kill" or "murder," should be applied to Hitler's massacres?

Would it make any difference either way?

There is so much of this terrible killing in the Bible that the commandment against killing is grotesquely meaningless. And if every person who fell into any of the condemned categories (idolaters, adulterers, etc.) had really been put to death, the total world population would then have been about fourteen.

Thou shalt not kill? You could have fooled me.

There are many more stories of massacres and torture in the Bible. These violent, barbaric stories are given short shrift by Christians, who mumble vaguely about how the stories are just histories of a barbarous age, not to be admired or emulated. Others distance themselves even further by declaring the stories to be symbolic only, not an accounting of real events.

But these sorts of explanations will not do. The Bible is purported to be the inspired word of God — every single word of it. Are we to understand that God couldn't come up with any less violent, less repulsive stories for his symbolic lessons? Is he such a limited author? Or, worse yet, do we assume that all of the atrocities and massacres did in fact occur, and at the command of God, as stated so clearly? If so, then God is as cruel and barbaric as any Hun who ever drew breath or sword.

A Killing Update

As Americans, we should have been real happy to hear that, according to General Norman Schwarzkopf, Theater Commander for Operation Desert Storm, God was on our side. (See Chapter Notes.) Isn't that great? God actually rolled up his sleeves and helped us kill 150,000 Iraqis. Of course, quite a few of our own people died, which is difficult to explain if God was really on our side. Then, too, someone had better inform Muslims everywhere that Allah, creator of the Koran, does not in fact exist, as proven by the outcome of the Gulf War, and that the real god, creator of the Bible, not only exists, but participates in killing humans. No matter which side you're talking about, this is not a comforting thought.

In a world that still contains religious fanatics with arsenals, the horrors of war will have to be a last-resort option exercised occasionally, at least until we humans grow up and find a better way to live. However, dragging God into the bloody business of war is an insult to all concerned. If there were a god, surely he would not choose sides in human killing. Turning God into a First Sergeant is also an insult to the women and men who deserve any and all credit for the outcome of any war. While soldiers have been claiming that God was on their side for as long as there have been wars, God did not win the Gulf War (if in fact any war can be said to be "won"). High technology and superior strategists did.

The idea that an all-powerful god chose to kill the loved ones of 500,000 or so Iraqis, is sickening. The idea that an all-powerful god would choose to kill *any* human beings is sickening. The idea of God The Murderer should offend even the least sensitive among us. And it should be obvious that such wholesale killing, by God and/or humans, clearly violates God's own directive, "Thou shalt not kill."

The Ten Or So Commandments

When was the last time you said "shalt?" When was the last time anyone said "shalt?" Aside from Shakespearean plays, that word disappeared from the English language a century ago. Yet when people quote the Bible's so-called Ten Commandments, "shalts" abound. There are of course revised editions of the Bible, but most people cling tenaciously to the King James Version, and in doing so they are engaging in a most subtle, but quite real, form of subterfuge. They are trying to cover up some mundane, often bizarre language with some fancy-sounding words in Ye Olde English. To a thinking person, this transparent tactic fails.

If these commandments, along with the rest of the Bible, are truly timeless, God-inspired words of wisdom, they do not need to be dressed up in archaic, Elizabethan English. They should stand very well on their own, even in the late 20th-century American English vernacular. Let's not forget that the Bible was originally written in Hebrew and Greek (and a smattering of

Aramaic) without a "shalt" to be found. King James' English is as extinct as the dinosaur and has no place in today's world. But this archaic English appears to impart more authority to the commandments. "Thou shalt not steal," for example, seems somehow more important than "Don't steal." The two directives are of course identical, but do they seem so?

So then, just the wording of the commandments, all by itself, gets us off to a bad start here. However, if we can set aside the awkward language (which is the result of Hebrew and Greek being translated into 17th-century English, an English most foreign to our eyes and ears) we can finally take a look at the commandments themselves.

Few people realize that there are not really ten commandments. There are anywhere from eleven to eighteen to hundreds, if you count every, single directive in the Old Testament. If you then add the commandments of the New Testament, such as "Thou shalt love thy neighbor as thyself" (Mark 12:31), you've got more. The most familiar ones, the Ten Commandments, recorded in Exodus 20, are ten in number only if you refer to some of the "thou shalts" as single entities while lumping others together to form only one commandment. The commandments recorded in Exodus 34 that were literally replacement commandments, since Moses apparently dropped and "breaketh" the original set, don't resemble the first set, even though God clearly states that they will: ". . . and I will write upon the tables the words that were in the first tables. . . ."

But have you ever heard a preacher exhorting his flock to keep the feast of weeks or to refrain from seething a kid in its mother's milk? Well, you certainly should have, since these are among the replacement commandments carefully recorded in the Bible. How could these two lists *possibly* not agree? Isn't God's word supposed to be infallible and unchangeable? If this omnipotent God dictated a set of replacement commandments, shouldn't they absolutely match the first set? But even if they don't, shouldn't they be as important as the first set, and observed with the same respect? Who arbitrarily decided that the first list was better than the second list? The whole thing reeks of mistranslations, interpolations, and just plain sloppiness, none of which should appear in a divinely inspired book.

Nevertheless, even if we accept, for no good reason, which is the only reason we have, that the first set of the Ten Commandments was the intended one, when the commandments are viewed as a whole, they are woefully lacking in moral guidance. Almost anyone, picked randomly from the phone book, could come up with a better set of rules to live by. The first half of these much-lauded commandments deals solely with how God is to be worshipped. Making graven images, for example, is forbidden, but more interesting, we are warned not to "have" any other gods. But if there aren't any other gods, how can they be had? It's like warning us not to have any other blue sky except for the one that's up there. Do we have any choice here? Obviously the warning is against the worship of false gods, but if they are false, then they clearly are not gods. The warning is oddly phrased.

But far more puzzling are the many activities *not* forbidden in these commandments. Killing, stealing, lying, adultery and coveting are the only "no-nos" mentioned. (The god who supposedly wrote these commandments, as well as his chosen favorites, so blatantly disregarded the commandment against killing as to make it meaningless. This topic is dealt with in great detail earlier in this chapter.)

An interesting omission that must rankle fundamentalists is abortion. Not only the Ten Commandments, but the entire Bible is silent on abortion. It never even mentions that it might not be the best thing to do. So while anti-abortionists scream and wave their Bibles, they do so foolishly, since there is no biblical authority for doing so. The best they can come up with is "Don't kill," the fetus supposedly being a human being.

Yet the Old Testament contains stories of the murders of hundreds of thousands of women, men and babies, all of whom are enthusiastically murdered at God's specific commands. Such stories force the commandment against killing to ring quite hollow in any context, and become preposterous with regard to abortion.

Coveting doesn't even belong on the same list as killing, nor does lying. Envy and lie-telling are not nice things, granted, but why forbid them when you don't even bother to forbid *rape*?! Ask any rape victim which she thinks is worse — telling lies or raping? Envying or raping?

Also not mentioned in the commandments, unbelievably, are cannibalism, slavery, child sexual abuse, wife-beating, assault & battery in general, torture, and kidnapping. "Thou shalt not sexually abuse a child" would have been a hell of a good commandment. How could these horrible crimes have been overlooked on such a list? Aren't these all a tad more serious than coveting your neighbor's Corvette?

The commandment that tells you not to covet, among other

things, your neighbor's wife, unabashedly and unambiguously makes it clear that a wife is a man's property, like a color TV. It also makes it clear that the Bible's readers were intended to be male only. And instead of worrying so much about whether or not your worshippers will remember your Sabbath day properly, how about forbidding slavery? What was God thinking about when he threw together this haphazard, woefully inadequate list of rules to guide human behavior?

Nor do the Big Ten urge people to love their children or to show kindness to others. Compassion gets short shrift in these commandments. Yet they are constantly referred to as the epitome of moral values and the perfect guidelines for living. But when you actually read them (all eleven, eighteen, six hundred and eighteen, or whatever) you realize that most of the terrible things people do to each other are not even mentioned. And our most vulnerable victims, our children, receive no special mention at all, except to be told to honor their parents. (Does that mean you must honor your father who has been raping you every day since you were five years old?) No, if you want to find some good old Family Values, you won't find them here. The commandments are a shabby, confusing deuce mixture of patriarchal and/or irrelevant directives. Profound they are not. In fact, if you were to sit down and try to come up with ten rules for humans to live by, your list is almost guaranteed to be better than the "Ten" Commandments. Try it and see.

As Foretold By The Prophets

Prophecy. We do like our prophets. Every year millions of us eagerly await the predictions made by people like Jeanne Dixon. A great many predictions, or prophecies, are ghoulishly horrendous, calling for calamities and shocking deaths. These are the ones we seem to like best. The more ghoulish, the better.

The only problem is that something like ninety-nine percent of these predictions do not come true. However, we seize onto the few that do, and then smugly hurl them at those skeptics who don't have open minds about such things. "See! She was right! There *was* a devastating hurricane in Florida!"

Whoa. I'm impressed. What I'm impressed with, though, is the amazing gullibility and lack of critical thinking needed to believe such things. There seems little doubt that today's appetite for tabloid predictions, horoscopes and UFO sightings is fueled by the same needs that permit our uncritical acceptance of religious beliefs. Any beliefs. And let's face it, we'll believe almost anything.

This craving for a belief system of some sort has always been with us, and you have to wonder why. It would seem that at some point in our evolutionary history, there must have been some advantage in having our minds open to all manner of beliefs, even silly ones. It does make sense, in a way, since rigid, inflexible minds would not be open to novel experimentation, one of our most adaptive traits. But everything has a price. And with our wonderfully flexible, open minds, always ready to accept new challenges, we also were ready to accept some rather impressive nonsense.

We eagerly embraced reincarnation (well, who wants to stay dead?) and gods who got real mad at us (where else did thunder and lightning come from?) and magic potions, lucky charms, hexes, leprechauns, witches . . . and prophets. Prophets were especially cool, because they could see into the future — a nifty talent, no doubt about it. And, not taking any chances, we believed what they told us.

The Bible is packed with prophets. That's plain to see. What is not so easy to see is just what those prophets were predicting. Christian fundamentalists, however, have no problems here. They possess their own powers of divination, or so it seems, because they can see crystal clear messages where the rest of us see arcane, convoluted, meaningless double-talk.

The author of the New Testament book of Matthew, whoever he was (no one knows), really had a flair for this prophecy thing. He saw fulfilled prophecies everywhere. In his absolute determination to link Jesus to prophecies in the Old Testament, he took incredible liberties. For example, the Old Testament book of Micah (chapter 5, verse 2) speaks of someone who will be coming to be ruler of Israel. The next few verses describe how this someone will protect Israel from the Assyrians who were preparing to "come into their land." What, you may ask, has this to do with Jesus? Well, nothing, actually. But Matthew twists and manipulates these words until he finally gets his much desired fulfilled prophecy about Jesus.

Actual verse from Micah: "But thou, Bethlehem Ephratah, though thou be little among the thousands of Judah, yet out of thee shall he come forth unto me that is to be ruler in Israel; whose goings forth have been from of old, from everlasting."

Is that crystal clear to you?

Here's what Matthew did with that verse: ". . . demanded of them where Christ should be born. And they said unto him,

In Bethlehem of Judea: for thus it is written by the prophet, And thou Bethlehem, in the land of Juda, art not the least among the princes of Juda: for out of thee shall come a Governor, that shall rule my people Israel." (Matthew 2:4–6)

What happened to Ephratah? Where did the "princes" come from? You can read those verses over and over, but you can never reconcile them. (Did Matthew think no one would notice that? Of course, since most people of his day were illiterate, perhaps he felt no one ever would.) Anyway, Matthew is claiming that the obscure reference in Micah is predicting the birth of Jesus some seven hundred years later. Yet the only relevant word in the entire Micah passage is "Bethlehem," and even that poses a problem. The way it is phrased, it could mean the *person* Bethlehem (such a person, descended from Ephratah, is mentioned in 1 Chronicles 2:51 & 4:4) or it could mean one of the clans of Judah. Over a half dozen translations of the Bible call it just that — a clan.

Since Micah refers to Bethlehem as little among "the thousands" of Judah, it could not possibly be a town, since Judah was far too small to have thousands of towns. Moreover, this much-lauded prophecy refers to a future ruler of Israel. Just when did Jesus become the ruler of Israel? His disciples numbered a mere dozen. The Jewish community as a whole paid Jesus no heed whatsoever, not then and not since. Ruler of Israel? Never.

Isaiah 7:14 is also proudly flaunted as an unambiguous prediction of the birth of Jesus: "Therefore the Lord himself shall give you a sign; Behold, a virgin shall conceive, and bear a son, and shall call his name Immanuel."

The problems here are that first, Isaiah clearly uses the Hebrew word "almah" for "young woman," and not the word "bethulah" that means virgin. Second, Mary did not name her son "Immanuel." Has no one noticed that? Third, if you read the entire chapter in Isaiah, it leaves no doubt that the son to be born was to be a sign to Ahaz, then sitting on the throne of Judah (approximately 700 B.C.). The sign was to be taken to mean that Judah would be safe from the power struggles then taking place in Ahaz' general area. The promised sign was to allay the fears of Ahaz. It had nothing to do with a child that was to be born some seven hundred years in the future.

But such are the extremes that Matthew had to go to in order to try to connect Jesus with the Old Testament. It is almost painful to observe his desperate attempts to relate the obviously unrelated passages.

Another supposedly fulfilled prophecy has to do with the destruction of a town named *Tyre* (also *Tyrus*). All you have to do to make this one work is to change the time period by a couple of centuries, and change the name Nebuchadnezzar to Alexander (as in "The Great," who *did* destroy Tyre) and Bingo! You've got yourself a fulfilled prophecy. (Ezekiel 26:7–14)

If a prophet wanted to predict that a Savior named Jesus was going to be born in a stable in the town of Bethlehem, during the reign of Tiberius, and that Jesus would have brown hair and a mole on his left cheek, then the prophet should have said that a Savior named Jesus was going to be born in a stable in Bethlehem, during the reign of Tiberius, and that Jesus would have brown hair and a mole on his left cheek. This is called prophecy.

Is this too much to ask of a holy prophet? Isn't it in fact the very *least* we should expect? You should not have to drag out your thesaurus, your dictionary, your almanac and your Guide to the Occult to figure out what the Bible is saying.

Jabberwocky

There is so much sheer nonsense in the Bible that there is almost too much to choose from when selecting examples. Touted as the greatest book ever written, the ultimate in divine wisdom, the Bible nevertheless possesses innumerable, indecipherable passages. The usual translation-error excuse, used so frequently by apologists, will not work with the following selections. You will quickly see why.

The prophets in the Bible were said to be "filled with the spirit of the Lord" when offering their pearls of wisdom. It may be that they were filled with other, more earthly spirits as they penned the following passages.

Please try to resist the temptation to skip over the following verses. Although lengthy biblical quotations are usually boring beyond belief, these, selected at random, are worth reading. There will be no accompanying commentary. The Bible's words will speak for themselves.

"And before the throne there was a sea of glass like unto crystal: and in the midst of the throne, and round about the throne, were four beasts full of eyes before and behind. And the first beast was like a lion, and the second beast like a calf, and the third beast had a face as a man, and the fourth beast was like a flying eagle. And the four beasts had each of them six wings

about them; and they were full of eyes within. . . ."
(Revelation 4:6–8)

❖ ❖ ❖

"And I beheld when he had opened the sixth seal, and, lo, there was a great earthquake; and the sun became black as sackcloth of hair, and the moon became as blood; And the stars of heaven fell unto the earth, even as a fig tree casteth her untimely figs, when she is shaken of a mighty wind. And the heaven departed as a scroll when it is rolled together. . . ."
(Revelation 6:12–14)

"And I looked, and, behold, a whirlwind came out of the north, a great cloud, and a fire infolding itself, and a brightness was about it, and out of the midst thereof as the colour of amber, out of the midst of the fire. Also out of the midst thereof came the likeness of four living creatures. And this was their appearance; they had the likeness of a man. And every one had four faces, and every one had four wings." (Ezekiel 1:4–6)

"Now as I beheld the living creatures, behold one wheel upon the earth by the living creatures, with his four faces. The appearance of the wheels and their work was like unto the colour of a beryl: and they four had one likeness: and their appearance and their work was as it were a wheel in the middle of a wheel. When they went, they went upon their four sides: and they turned not when they went. As for their rings, they were so high that they were dreadful; and their rings were full of eyes round about them four. And when the living creatures went, the wheels went by them: and when the living creatures were lifted up from the earth, the wheels were lifted up."

(Ezekiel 1:15–19)

❖ ❖ ❖

"And I saw an angel standing in the sun; and he cried with a loud voice, saying to all the fowls that fly in the midst of heaven, Come and gather yourselves together unto the supper of the great God; That ye may eat the flesh of kings, and the flesh of captains, and the flesh of mighty men, and the flesh of horses, and of them that sit on them, and the flesh of all men, both free and bond, both small and great."

(Revelation 19:17,18)

And so on. Is any of this stuff supposed to mean something? And do you suppose that these writers were perhaps smoking those "funny" cigarettes as they wrote? If God's prophets had something to tell us, we should be able to understand, easily, what that something is. Apparitions with four faces and four wings mean nothing, absolutely nothing, to a normal human being. Just as with mental telepathy and palm-reading, prophecy fulfillment depends entirely on how you categorize a "hit" and a "miss." If any of the above can be categorized as prophesying *anything*, then there is no such thing as a "miss."

There are bizarre explanations of these bizarre prophecies. The European Common Market is in there somewhere, and the beasts somehow refer to the strife in the Middle East. The flesh-eating part is less obvious, but has to do either with the generally bad stuff in the world or with the Donner Party. The unbelievable latitude in the Christian interpretations makes it possible for anyone to be a prophet. Just compose any odd sentence such as, "The moon will spread her wings when the seven beasts have undone the scrolls of yesterday," and then sit back and wait for something in the newspaper to strike your fancy. Then, force your meaning into that news article and Presto! You may claim clairvoyance.

Still, we're supposed to believe that all of the preceding nonsense was provided to us by God-inspired, honest-to-goodness prophets. The only problem is that they didn't also provide us with the necessary, magic decoder rings to go with the prophecies.

Eternal truths from an all-knowing god? I think not.

4

The Genesis Of Absurdity

When God throws the dice are loaded.

Greek Proverb

In the Beginning . . . so many books and articles have that title, echoing the first words in the Bible. It seems a most logical place to start — in the beginning. But if you look closely at the creation story in the book of Genesis, you'll find that you will be amazed, amused or angry. But you will not be bored.

Twinkle, Twinkle, Little Star

Perhaps nowhere is the human ego more spotlighted than in the biblical account of creation. In it, God creates Heaven and Earth, day and night, and all living things. And "man" was to have "dominion" over "every creeping thing that creepeth upon the earth." (Interestingly, to this day, we have yet to dominate the cockroach.) As if such arrogant assumptions were not enough for us, Genesis proceeds to inform us that on the fourth day of creation God created the sun, the moon and the stars, all simply for our benefit. Just how there could have been three prior days and nights, with alternating lightness and darkness, before the sun was even created, is just one of countless biblical absurdities.

The fact that fundamentalists are making *any* inroads at all in having this nonsense taught in schools as science, chills the very hearts of those dedicated to the separation of church and state. If we are going to teach "creation science" (a contradiction in terms) as an alternative to evolution, then we should also teach the stork theory as an alternative to biological reproduction. The two scenarios are completely analogous.

Important here is the point that the stars received third billing in this creationist heavenly light show, and were supposedly set "in the firmament of the heaven to give light upon the earth," along with the sun and the moon. (Genesis 1:17)

What makes this assertion so absurd is that 99.9999% of the stars in the sky are not even visible from Earth. So how could they possibly have been set in the heaven to give light upon the Earth? They don't "give" any light upon the Earth. They don't give any light at all that is detectable by humans, except to the Hubble Telescope, now silently orbiting the Earth. And even Hubble can't distinguish individual stars in the vast majority of the billions of far-flung galaxies. On Earth, we are blind to the stars.

While many have poked fun at astronomer Carl Sagan's description of the billions and billions of stars just in our own galaxy, he is nevertheless quite correct in his description, just as he is correct in his characterization of our universe as containing billions and billions of galaxies. Hubble has backed him up all the way. But we are uncomfortable with these numbers. Most of us have trouble imagining what one million dollars in currency would look like sitting on the kitchen table. How much *is* a million? Could any of us even count that far from memory alone? It's doubtful. So when you start throwing around numbers like a few hundred billion, our eyes glaze over and we hope someone will change the subject. The numbers are just too big.

In addition to the understandable human problem of grasping astronomical numbers, there is the more fundamental problem of reassessing our importance in this universe if *most* of the universe is invisible to us. This means that we are equally invisible to *most* of the universe. What a humbling thought. We, whom Genesis describes as the lords of all creation, are not even a freckle on its face. This is where we balk at considering the Cosmos.

Our possible insignificance gets in the way of our contemplation of the vastness of the universe. It was also the driving force behind all of the world's religious creation myths, which place humans smack in the center of creation. *"It's all for us !"* we told ourselves as we wrote our creation stories. To think otherwise is to question our importance, an act of treachery few of us ever have been guilty of. God says we're important, so we're important. Don't confuse the issue with billions and billions of galaxies. Please.

These billions of galaxies are not even hinted at in the Bible, since its writers held the primitive flat-earth-with-lights-revolving-around-it theory. In fact, the word "firmament" translates from the Hebrew as something like "beaten metal lid," like a frying pan cover. Biblical authors actually believed that if you could somehow get up there high enough in the sky, and then flicked your finger against the "firmament," you would hear a "thunk."

Today fundamentalists are uncomfortable with discoveries in astronomy, since every new discovery makes their biblical creation science seem more and more primitive and wholly inappropriate in any classroom. So it is not so surprising that many people still choose not to believe that Apollo astronauts ever set foot on the moon. That history-making event was the thin edge of the wedge, so to speak, since it opened up the possibility of space travel. But, more important, it opened up the possibility that there might be places worth traveling *to*. Other worlds. Other beings, perhaps. And where, then, would that leave us in the universal pecking order? We are still very much obsessed with pecking order, and any possible extraterrestrial intelligence might topple us from our perceived position at the top. So we close our eyes to what might be "out there" as well as to humankind's stunning achievement in the Apollo Program.

Have you ever noticed that among those who claim that space aliens have in fact already visited Earth, there is a pervasive common theme? The aliens, they say, are positively fascinated by us. They apparently can't get enough of us, and feel the need to prod and probe our naked bodies. My, we're fascinating. Never mind that these alien beings, as space-faring creatures, would necessarily have seen wonders unimaginable to us, rendering our own physiology quite mundane. Never mind that the most logical place for a space ship to land and say hello would be on the White House lawn, not in Rat's Rear, New Mexico. Never mind the absurdity of the proposition that these obviously superior beings, who have mastered space-travel, journeying millions or billions of light-years, suddenly develop carburetor trouble or something when they reach Earth, forcing crash landings. Ignore these things, ignoring logic as you do so, and you are then free to exclaim, "Space aliens are interested in *us!* They exist for *us!*" We do go on and on like a broken record.

It should be immediately apparent that the same ego that prompts space-alien stories also prompted the various creation myths that place humans squarely at center stage. The biblical story of creation clashes unavoidably with our expanding knowledge of the Cosmos. And this is the rub. This is where science locks horns with religion. Science seeks to understand the world around us by discovering the diverse, verifiable laws of nature. Religion seeks to keep blinders on us, holding sacred that which is ancient simply *because* it is ancient. Religion cannot accommodate change, whereas science thrives on it. The Catholic Church only recently admitted its unconscionably cruel and unbelievably stupid treatment of Galileo.

Voltaire was right on the money when he said that if God had not existed it would have been necessary for humans to invent him. But he was talking two centuries before the Apollo moon landings. Our horizons have broadened unbelievably since then, even beyond Voltaire's fertile imaginings. Where our rocket thrusters will ultimately send us is unknowable at the moment, but the possibilities certainly stir the blood.

If we can crawl out of the cradle of our primitive religious myths, we can open our eyes, look skyward, and see what's really out there. And if there *is* life out there, a probability more likely than not, even if life is as rare as it so far appears to be in our own solar system, then our earthly gods, who are credited with only earthly concerns, will be forced into their rightful places as human ego-indicators. And nothing more. And our humanity will be all the more precious for its uniqueness.

But if we should discover, somehow, some day, that life exists nowhere else in the universe, it still will not argue for our many primitive, mutually exclusive, suspiciously human gods. The God of Genesis will still be beyond resuscitation. What such a discovery would mean, however, is that we would then be able to state, with a lonely certainty, that life is more precious than we realized.

Either way, with or without other life in the universe, such discoveries will be cause for human celebration. By then we will have shed our quaint notions of an earthly god who set the "tiny," twinkling stars in our sky just so our ancestors wouldn't bump into each other on a moonless night. And we will be able to marvel at the vastness and the beauty of our universe, free of the constraints of our Earth-bound gods.

The Eve Thing

The Genesis story of Adam and Eve and the serpent and the apple, is one of the best known stories in the Western World. It ranks right up there with Jack and the Beanstalk, Peter Pan, and Noah's Ark. And they are all equally true.

The funny thing about the apple part of the story is that an apple is never mentioned anywhere in the Genesis account of humanity's "downfall." "Fruit of the tree" is all that is mentioned, and since fig leaves are mentioned in this same story, the tree was probably a sycamore fig. To Westerners, though, the apple is far more familiar, while figs and dates, although very well known in the Middle East, are more alien. It is another example of rewriting history to suit your personal tastes.

But whatever fruit is involved, the idea of the God of Creation planting a special tree in the middle of the Garden of Paradise for the sole purpose of tempting, possibly fatally, the people he had just created, is diabolically cruel. It is a classic case of entrapment. But to what end?

So the God of all creation, all-powerful and all-knowing, outwits two of his own creations. Are we supposed to be impressed here? Was it really a challenge? More important, was it really a surprise? Did this all-knowing god (who supposedly knew all things past, present and future) not know exactly how this little drama would unfold?

Supposedly God gave Adam and Eve permission to eat of every tree in the Garden of Eden except one. Referred to as the "tree of the knowledge of good and evil," this tree was absolutely forbidden. So why did God put it there in the first place? That question deserves an answer. Aside from toying with his new creations, the way a cat might play with a mouse, there seems to be no good reason for the entire tree-fruit-eat-sin episode. Setting someone up for failure is unkind and unworthy of any god, especially when you consider that Adam and Eve were supposedly ordinary people, just like you and me. Do you suppose the God of all creation had an edge in this battle of wits?

And just where did the serpent come from? It was supposedly a serpent who tempted Eve, by *talking* to her, into eating the forbidden fruit. (This really is a silly story. How can people believe it?) Anyway, who created this serpent? If God created all things, as stated in this same book of Genesis, then obviously God created the evil serpent. But why? The cat and mouse scenario comes to mind again.

Supposedly, though, the serpent tempts Eve, Eve gives in and eats the fruit, then Eve tempts Adam and Adam gives in, then God finds out about it (as if he didn't already know) and then God curses both of them for giving in. Thus we have the downfall of humankind, and from that day forward humanity was condemned, by God, to suffer from sin and misery. We really blew it.

Before the Fall, Adam and Eve didn't notice they were naked. How could they not have noticed that? Before the Fall, childbirth was apparently not such a painful thing. How could that have been? Before the Fall, everything was perfect and wonderful. But if God hadn't created that absurd serpent and that equally absurd tree, things would have *stayed* perfect and wonderful. So why did he do that?

It's difficult to scrutinize such preposterous stories, as if they were real, because everything you say about such stories ends up sounding as silly as the stories. However, this particular story must be looked at because of its very important underlying message. That underlying message has been the root cause of endless suffering by women at the hands of men for thousands of years. You see, Eve was the one who screwed up first, so Eve caused humanity's downfall.

That theme has been pounded into us ad nauseam, by men predominantly, since the Bible was first put into writing. But no one ever, till recently, bothered to pose the obvious question. If Eve was the fool and Adam the wise, why did Adam give in at all? Why does Eve take the entire rap for the wrongdoing of both of them? Did a little human bias somehow sneak into this story?

Eve's sin has been used to justify the withholding of painkillers during childbirth, since God cursed her with the pain of childbirth. It has been used to cast all women as temptresses, removing from men any responsibility for their own sexual activities, including rape. (She was "asking" for it, remember?) This continues to be used to justify the horrific mutilations that are performed on young girls, even as this is being written, where sharp knives are used to slice off clitorises. It is used to justify the sewing shut of young girls' vaginal lips (causing all sorts of excruciatingly painful infections) so that no intercourse can take place until the men in these girls' lives decide who owns which girls.

In fact, for centuries, this Eve Thing has been used as an all-purpose, generic biblical authority for the sit-down-and-shut-up kind of male dominance so familiar to us all. To be sure, other cultures have managed to achieve first-rate forms of total male dominance, even without any snake and apple stories. But for Westerners, the Eve Thing has been the bedrock of male dominance, and fundamentalists even today do not want to let go of this heavenly carte blanche for committing all manner of crimes against women. It is even brought up in the preposterously inappropriate context of the subject of equal pay for women. It has indeed been a useful tool for men.

But it is time for all of us to grow up, put away these childish tales, and learn to respect and love each other. This will only serve to make life more pleasant for all of us. It is time we put the serpent-and-Eve Thing to rest.

Murder, God Wrote

One of the very first things to occur in the Bible is a murder. There are 1,189 chapters in the Bible and by Chapter 4 a murder takes place. It follows immediately on the heels of the creation of the first human beings. And it is not just your ordinary, everyday murder here. It is a brother killing his only other brother. And it is not just one brother killing another brother. It is one-quarter of the world's population killing another one-quarter of the world's population. This is one spectacular murder. It is also impossible to believe.

The first two people in the world, Adam and Eve, supposedly had two children, Cain and Abel, and the first thing Cain did was kill Abel. Why? Those four people had the whole world to themselves, literally. Was it just not big enough for the four of them? How could they conceivably have got on each other's nerves to the point of someone committing a murder? It's nonsensical.

God delivers a little speech to Cain after the murder, in which he (God) says that he will "set a mark upon Cain, lest any finding him should kill him." (Genesis 4:15) *Who* might find him? After he murdered his brother, there were no other people on the entire planet Earth at the time, except for Mom and Dad. So who could possibly find and kill Cain?

After the murder, Cain journeys into the land of Nod. God punished Cain by making him a vagabond forever, whatever that means. (Considering, though, the rest of the blood-spattered pages of the Old Testament, it seems Cain got off easy here.) But as soon as he arrives in Nod, he "knows" his wife and she bears him a son. Now where on Earth did *she* come from? She wasn't there one verse ago. So who exactly was this wife? Was it a sister? His own mother? A different animal species? Who?

This Adam and Eve story is totally implausible, as well as being very distasteful, since incest is required to make it work. As an allegory, it might perhaps make some sense, if all it represented were the literary efforts of an ancient people struggling to explain their even more ancient origins. Cain might represent the origins of agriculture, for example, while Abel might represent the more primitive, less civilized nomadic tribes who tended their animal flocks. But as a real, honest-to-goodness accounting of how human beings came to exist on Earth, it is poppycock.

And more disturbing, the key part of this story is a murder. People hadn't even been around long enough to become familiar with their surroundings on this newly created Earth and already they're killing each other. There is simply far too much killing in the Bible. You have to wonder why there are no recountals of kindnesses, or tender moments between these first humans, who were supposedly created in "God's image." The only interactions related in this tale are sexual intercourse, jealousy, and murder.

As early as Chapter 7 in this same first book of the Bible, God is so ticked off with the people he created, that he sends a flood to kill every single person on Earth, now numbering in the many thousands, except for one lucky family on an Ark. And except for that one boat full of people and animals, God did indeed kill every living thing on the planet Earth.

Very shortly after the Flood, God gets worried about how humans are becoming rather uppity, as they begin building a tower that will supposedly reach all the way up to Heaven. (Genesis 11) So God scuttles this endeavor by causing all of the people working on the tower to suddenly begin speaking in different languages, so they can't understand each other. And naturally they have to stop working on the tower. Hence the name "Tower of Babel." Thus, supposedly, were languages born.

The idea that a building could reach Heaven is childish. It betrays a very primitive world-view. But the idea quite obviously seemed plausible to the writers of the Bible. Were they perhaps influenced by the pyramids? In any event, these biblical writers didn't have a clue as to how "high" the sky really is. This is another very silly story.

Likewise, the origins of different languages are explained by having God *zap* them all into existence at one time, in one place, another equally unbelievable concept. Languages evolved over great areas and great time spans by multitudinous cultures. But since these isolated biblical writers could only dimly guess at their own history, the Tower of Babel story came into existence.

In Chapter 19 of Genesis, we find that God is again angry

with the way people are behaving. (We must ask again, if God wanted perfect people, why didn't he just create perfect people? Since nothing is impossible for an omnipotent god, that question demands an answer.) God was angry with the people living in the cities of Sodom and Gomorrah so he decided to kill them all. Women, men, children, everyone, was going to die. Even the plants that grew out of the ground were going to be destroyed. And, they were. One of God's "favorites," Lot, was saved from the carnage. But Lot's wife, after being told not to look back at the cities being destroyed, did so anyway. Her punishment was that God turned her into a pillar of salt.

Aside from the serious theological problems attendant upon a God who is constantly killing people because they anger him, thereby making a mockery of the purported benevolence of this loving, merciful god, there is the overall silliness of these stories to contend with.

These stories are the stuff of fever dreams and psychedelic drugs. The create-and-destroy theme is very disturbing, and betrays a bad-tempered god, prone to violent fits of rage. Yet fundamentalists insist that these stories represent the real, actual history of our lovely, blue planet, and portray a merciful, loving god. How do they portray a merciful, loving god?

Global flood? Impossible. Horrendous local flood? Very possible. There have *always* been horrendous local floods. Fire and brimstone rained down by a wrathful god? Impossible. Violent volcanic eruption? Very possible. There have *always* been violent volcanic eruptions. Languages evolved all over the planet, as linguists very well know. And the pillar of salt story is too silly to discuss further.

When It Rains, It Pours

The story of Noah's Ark and the Great Flood is a real thorn in the side of Christian fundamentalists. Aside from the monumental problem of just where Noah found penguins and polar bears in Palestine, not to mention kangaroos and three-toed sloths, there is the problem of dropping all of these creatures off at their native lands after the flood was over.

Gathering up a male and female of each of the tens of thousands of species of butterflies, to mention only one insect, must have been a tricky business. There are well over a million known species of insects in all, and supposedly, male and female collected he them. Somehow, he had to find a way to feed all these creatures, and then he had to figure out how to keep them from eating each other. (Or him.) Koalas, for one example of a fussy eater, will only eat fresh Eucalyptus leaves. And lions, of course, will only eat other animals. How many tons of feed would be required and how much space would be required to store it all?

The enormous amounts of dung that would necessarily have been produced would have had to be dealt with somehow. How did they dispose of all that dung without making everyone seriously ill? Consider, too, that the earth was supposedly flooded to a height of nearly five miles with rain water. Marine life could not possibly survive if that tremendous amount of fresh rain water were added to the Earth's oceans. So how did they survive? And what did the animals eat after they were let out on land again, land that no longer supported living plants due to the inundation?

These practical, unanswerable questions abound by the dozens. But the larger, philosophical question is even more unsettling. How could a loving, all-merciful god send a flood to destroy his own creations? The image of all of the world's babies, toddlers and pregnant women treading water until they drown is not a pleasant one.

This grisly, impossible scenario of the entire Earth being flooded is supposed to be a truthful, actual event in spite of the uninterrupted histories of China and Egypt. (See Chapter Notes.) These cultures recorded events that took place during the same time period in which the supposed Flood took place. Yet they make no reference to any such flood. You'd think they would have noticed.

Equally bizarre and totally contrary to the laws of nature is the purported creation of the rainbow at this time. Following the Flood, God supposedly put the rainbow "in the clouds" as a "covenant" between himself and humans, and to remind him of the temper tantrum he had just thrown. (And killing every woman, man, child and animal on the planet Earth, except for a scanty handful, certainly remains unchallenged as the Blue-Ribbon, All-Around Champion of temper tantrums.) The beauty of this newly created rainbow was supposed to help prevent God from committing a similar wholesale slaughter in the future, such massacres by this loving god apparently resting on a hair-trigger.

But the point is that a rainbow is a simple matter of the right combination of light and water, and rainbows came into existence as soon as there *was* light and water. The story of its creation after the Flood confirms the extremely primitive nature of this story, even as an allegory.

This supposed flood causes much mischief among today's fundamentalists who somehow must try to present the impossible as possible without sounding ridiculous.

Open Your Books To Chapter One

Rationalists can only shake their heads in dismay and wonder if these primitive stories will ever fade away and properly join the ranks of mythical folklore. The scary alternative is that they will somehow be forced into our classrooms as creation science, that ultimate oxymoron, taking a huge gouge out of our Constitution in the process. If such an improper, Christianity-sponsoring, unconstitutional thing should come to pass, and these incredible stories end up being presented in our classrooms, then the Creation Story must be told in its entirety. No tactical editing should be allowed. The biblical story of scientific creationism would therefore have to include all of the following:

(1) The fact that the Bible states clearly that there were three days and three nights before the sun had been created. This must be explained in science class.

(2) The fact that there are two contradictory accounts in Genesis about the creation of Adam and Eve. One version has Adam and Eve being created simultaneously. A mere eleven verses later, Adam is described as being created alone, then ultimately put to sleep, during which time God removes one of his ribs and makes a woman, Eve, out of that rib. Both stories about the creation of Adam and Eve, as told in the book of Genesis, must be presented, even though each version positively contradicts the other. And the contradictions must be explained.

(3) In scientific terms, the creation of a woman from a man's rib must be explained.

(4) Whether or not Adam was created with testicles must be addressed. If he was created alone, with no human female anywhere on Earth, why would he have been created with testicles? If it was because God knew he was soon going to create Eve, then why not create them simultaneously in the first place? Other than trying to prove that men are more important than women, separate creations make no sense. Creationists must explain this glaring problem.

(5) If an all-powerful god did not want Adam and Eve to be such wicked sinners, it must be explained why they turned out that way, anyway.

(6) Where in fact did Cain find a wife to help propagate the human species? The abrupt appearance of Cain's wife, literally out of nowhere, must be explained, assuming he didn't marry his own sister or his own mother. Cain's wife must be explained in a way that eliminates incest. If God was creating people elsewhere at that time, why doesn't Genesis record such an important event?

(7) The Flood and Noah's supposed Ark must be presented in any creation story, since all of us alive today, with our wildly divergent racial and ethnic differences, are supposedly descended from this one man's family. In addition, it must be explained how we traveled to every part of the globe, filling the world with people, in only a couple of thousand years. Noah's prolific offspring must also be explained in a way that eliminates incest.

(8) Since creationism, denying evolution, is intended to ex-

plain the origin of life on Earth, some explanation must be offered as to how life rejuvenated itself on the newly flood-damaged, totally barren land that would have been all that remained after the Flood.

(9) The origins of languages must be explained.

All in all, it seems there is a lot of explaining to do. But if creationists want to tell their religious story to our schoolchildren as science, then they must tell *all* of it. Anything less would be mere proselytizing rather than educating. And of course all of us, believers as well as nonbelievers, agree that our classrooms should be intended solely to educate. Correct?

5

Sex And Satan

. . . for it is never lawful to exclude the primary end of marriage which is the procreation of children.

Saint Francis de Sales,
Introduction to the Devout Life

If the Religious Right is right, someone is having far too much sex these days. There are teenage pregnancies, shotgun weddings, sex in the cinema, sex on TV, and hookers everywhere. Sex, sex, sex. Satan, supposedly, is at the bottom of all this. And, as that wonderful song from that wonderful stage play shockingly informed us, Texas has a whorehouse in it! That'll set you back on your heels, won't it?

There is something out of tune in this chorus of denunciation here. Christians harp about the lusts of the flesh and the sins of sex. But *someone* is keeping all those hookers busy, and it isn't a handful of atheists living on the outskirts of town. Those ladies of the night have plenty of work to keep them busy, and their clientele cannot all be Televangelists. So either the polls are wrong when they inform us that eighty to ninety percent of Americans are True Believers, or else True Believers don't consider sex to be all that evil. If they truly considered it evil, they wouldn't do it so much. In either case, why don't Christian proselytizers shut up already about sex, and turn their attention to important matters — like starving babies? Now there's a subject worth getting in a muck sweat about. But sex?

The embarrassingly disingenuous argument that sex is meant to be only for the creation of precious life is just that. Embarrassingly disingenuous. When you are sexually aroused, babies and diapers are the absolute furthest thing from your mind. And if life were really all that special and precious, it shouldn't be so easy to get it started in the back seat of an old Chevy, as you steam up the windows. A bag of French fries and a six-pack of Bud, and a new life is on its way. That's precious and special?

Of course sex *was* created to ensure the arrival of babies. So Mother Nature had to make it very appealing to ensure those babies. And appealing it is. But the actual, physical act of intercourse is preceded by feelings and emotions wholly unrelated to increasing the world population. The desire to have a bouncing baby, no matter how strong the desire, is never going to produce a male erection. Erotica will. Like it or not, this is how humans function.

Woody Allen's hilarious statement aside ("Do you think sex is dirty? It is if you're doing it right.") there is no reason for the Christian Right, or anyone else, to keep harping about how dirty sex is. Sex isn't dirty. It's fun. Of all the bad things that happen in this world, *responsible* sex is the least of our problems.

There can be no doubt that AIDS and other sexually transmitted diseases must be regarded as the serious health threats that they are. Our current overpopulation is exhausting our resources as it is, but combined with our staggering growth rate, there is real reason for alarm. So sex carries with it some very serious responsibilities and imperatives. The terrible irony, though, is that even though the condom is one of the best methods for preventing pregnancy and the spread of STDs, the Catholic Church is fervently preaching *against* the use of condoms, for any reason, at any time.

People are dying of AIDS. No one, so far, has survived it. Hopefully that will change soon, but in the meantime, condoms are one of the most effective means of at least minimizing the chances of contracting this killer virus. So for the Pope to preach against condoms is tantamount to preaching the death penalty for engaging in sexual intercourse. Death for sex? This is unconscionable.

Wanton, irresponsible sexual behavior is one thing. But the ferocious, religious attacks on sex per se are unjustified. It's time to stop this nonsense. Sexuality is a key part of our humanity and religions have historically made far too big a fuss about it. Let's put this thing in perspective.

Here Comes The Bride

There is a tragic irony in Christianity's preachings about the American Family ("the family that prays together stays together") and women suffer the most because of it. The Bible goes to great lengths denouncing the "evils of the flesh." Lust is truly a four-letter word. Diatribes against and warnings about whores, whoring and whoredom abound in profusion. Allegories, metaphors, similes and parables are overflowing with references to playing the whore and playing the harlot. The word "woman" is hurled as an insult.

". . . and they have caused Egypt to err in every work thereof, as a drunken man staggereth in his vomit. . . in that day shall Egypt be like unto women. . . ." (Isaiah 19:14, 16)

A woman is "unclean" during and after her periods. She is unclean after childbirth. She is unclean after having sex and so is the man who had sex with her. Fornication will lead you straight to Hell. Childbirth will be agonizing because God wants it that way. It's a woman's punishment for being the same sex as Eve. So says the Bible.

By the time a properly programmed Christian girl arrives at her wedding night, virginal and God-fearing, the least likely thing to happen is the awakening of a healthy, natural sexuality. After listening, year after year, to the graphic condemnation of the evils of the flesh, the lusts of the body and the uncleanness of her own body, a young woman has almost no option but to view the act of sex with mingled horror, shame, distaste and guilt. How could it be otherwise? She is expected to believe that lusting is evil, and her body is unclean a good deal of the time, and the agony of childbirth is a curse upon her by her god. She is to believe that if she were to have sex with her betrothed three hours before the wedding it would be a vile, evil, lusting sin of the flesh for which she would deserve damnation. Then, three hours after the wedding, she is supposed to turn into a sex kitten. Guess again.

The family that prays together stays together? Well, maybe. But married men do not have affairs or seek out the company of prostitutes because they aren't getting enough praying at home. One of the strongest components of a happy marriage is a healthy sex life, but if a girl learns to equate sex with evil and her body with uncleanness, a healthy sex life is impossible for her.

Men suffer as well, in that they may come to view their virginal brides as holy and pure, the Madonna complex, and sex with a saint just doesn't work. After his wife has given birth to his child, a husband's problem may get worse. After all, you can't do *those* things to a mother, for heaven's sake, especially to the mother of your own child. Most men want to do all manner of *those* things, however, and if they view their wives as some sort of combination of revered mothers and cherished saints, their search for excitement will take place outside the home. If you further compound this problem by prohibiting birth control, you are signing the death warrant for satisfactory marital sex. If, along with everything else, marital sex results in a never-ending series of pregnancies, the marriage bed will be uninviting in the extreme.

The Bible's whole attitude toward women is blatantly sexist. Its supposedly holy men collected women like baseball trading cards, having hundreds of wives and concubines, sending the very clear message that women are property. The tenth commandment openly refers to them as property. And the pronouncements about a woman being unclean because of her natural bodily functions seem to border on the phobic. A woman is not unclean after she gives birth. She is tired. She may also be depressed and determined never to go through *that* again, but she is not unclean. Nor do her monthly menstrual discharges make her so. If natural body functions are to be viewed as clean or unclean, a peculiar idea to begin with, then a woman's monthly discharge can't hold a candle to your average 165-pound man's daily discharge of feces.

The whole business could be dismissed as silly and unimportant if it were not for the far-reaching effects such attitudes have on women. A woman's self-esteem is systematically eroded by these characterizations, and shame and guilt come to dominate a woman's view of her own body. Mental health it is not. So the very teachings that are supposed to keep families together serve instead to drive them inexorably apart, and this is tragic.

The Roman Catholic Church has probably contributed more misery in this area than any other single institution. Its Church Fathers spent centuries pondering such mysteries as why God created woman at all, since another man would have been the logical choice for Adam's companion, intellectually, spiritually and in every other aspect of human existence. However, men can't have babies. So that's why we have to have women.

These same Fathers also wrestled with the problem of just how sinful marital sex really was, now a mortal sin, now a venial sin, and settled uneasily on vigorously condemning the pleasure in the act, while grudgingly acknowledging the necessity of having the act if the world is to have people in it. Even when conception is the only goal for intercourse, taking pleasure in that intercourse is a sin, and of course if conception is not the only goal, then intercourse is forbidden altogether. At one point in history the penance for coitus interruptus (pulling out before ejaculation) was more severe than that for murder. Contraception was considered to *be* murder, and clerics actually contemplated whether or not a serious sin could be said to take place if "pulling out" occurred because the house caught on fire, or a murderer broke into the house.

For quite some time the Church believed that the soul entered the male embryo at forty days and the female embryo at eighty days, females being simply flawed males.

Sex is filthy, celibacy is the only pure state of being (although how that San Francisco group of gay priests with AIDS can honestly call themselves celibate is a mystery) and trying to prevent the birth of more babies than you can feed will send you straight to Hell. So says the Catholic Church. Have those babies, year after year, and if they starve to death so be it, but if you use a condom Hell awaits.

The pleasure-hating celibates (or proclaimed celibates) of the Catholic Church have so permeated moral theology that as recently as 1980 the Pope referred to adultery with one's own wife, which the early Fathers railed against century after century. Adultery with one's own wife means enjoying it. If you have a good time your wife is a harlot. Moral theologian Fritz Tillman in 1940, and Cardinal Faulhaber in 1936, both agreed with Hitler that reproduction among inferior, handicapped, hereditary-disease-imparting humans (Faulhaber called them "vermin") should be banned. Hitler wanted to implement forced sterilization, but these two pillars of Catholic morality objected. Why? Because sterilization would allow these defectives to have the sinful pleasure of sex without the burden of parenthood that *must* accompany sex. According to Tillman, this was the "gravest moral objection" to Hitler's proposal of sterilizing these "defective" humans. Neither theologian objected to removing these "vermin" from the rest of the genetically pure population by locking them away from society, in concentration camps, for as long as they were capable of reproduction.

So here we have the disgusting specter of two highly respected, 20th-century Roman Catholic leaders disagreeing with Hitler's proposed obscenity only because it would allow these wretches to have the fun of sex without the worry of babies. They had no problem with Adolph and his concentration camps, but they would not tolerate worry-free orgasms. This is sickening stuff.

But there's more.

In 1587, in an effort to thwart "filthy lasciviousness," the Pope decreed that eunuchs could not marry. Even if a man could have an erection and ejaculate a semen-like fluid, if he was lacking testicles the wedding was off. No babies, no marriage. The serious theological debates that raged around testicles, semen, erections and pulling out, all failed to acknowledge the difference between the human capacity for mutually passionate, caring lovemaking, and the simple ability to reproduce like cockroaches. This disgraceful disregard for human dignity remained as policy until 1977, when the Church finally lifted the ban on the marriages of eunuchs. (It is difficult to believe that this is a discussion of religion, but it is.)

In 1982 the Catholic Church denied a 25-year-old man with muscular atrophy permission to marry, and as recently as 1996 a Catholic bishop rejected the marriage application of a paraplegic on the grounds of impotency. No erection, no marriage.

Could there be a more degrading view of married love?

(Just why the Pope, a supposed lifelong celibate, should be dictating sexual conduct in the first place, is a bit of a mystery. As someone has quipped, "If the Pope knows anything about sex, he shouldn't.")

And finally, in 1988, the Catholic Church decreed that a hemophiliac with AIDS may never, ever have intercourse with his wife because the use of a condom is forbidden. If the hemophiliac simply cannot abstain, then it would be better for him to infect his wife with AIDS, thus sentencing her to a certain early death, than to use a condom. The Church has spoken.

Just what does all this mean? The not-at-all-hidden agenda here is simply that women stink. Contact with them should be avoided at all costs, celibacy being the loftiest of all possible goals. But this degrading view, aside from being just plain asinine, also presents a religious puzzle. If sex is such an affront to God, so often described by these Church Fathers as filthy, base, degrading, sinful, vile, wanton, and on and on, why didn't God create us to reproduce like viruses or bacteria? If God can do anything, asexual reproduction would have been simple to arrange, and women could have been dispensed with altogether, which undoubtedly would have pleased those early Church Fathers no end.

If the functions of the testicles and ovaries are disgusting enough to offend God, then why did he create them? What kind of sadist would create a powerful sex drive in people and then threaten them with Hell if they respond to it? Are we to imagine a god who, after creating this thing called sexual desire, sits back watching and laughing up his sleeve as we poor mortals fail in our struggle to defeat that which God himself created?

Jerome, Augustine, Aquinas, and all the other early Church Fathers may have imagined just such a god, but such thoughts are completely unacceptable today. Perhaps we should assume that all of this pathological, phobic, woman-hating rubbish is just that: pathological, phobic, woman-hating rubbish.

By declaring birth control a sin, the Catholic Church makes all sexual intercourse a game of Russian Roulette. Catholic women are faced with three untenable choices.

(1) Become a breeding machine and endure fifteen or twenty pregnancies in your lifetime, during which time a healthy, happy sex life is absolutely impossible. (2) Engage in sex only on the most severely restricted basis, which is still no guarantee against pregnancy since the so-called Rhythm Method doesn't work but it may limit the number of pregnancies you must endure. Such severe restrictions, however, will frustrate you and your husband, making a healthy, happy sex life absolutely impossible. (3) Practice birth control anyway, knowing that you are "sinning" against God. You can now have sex freely but every time you do you will be aware of the "sinful" nature of the act, making a healthy, happy sex life absolutely impossible. Some choices. And, of course, the inevitable tragic result of this dilemma will be unwanted children.

If these dismal birth control choices seem depressing, consider the Catholic woman who is also a battered wife. She is also faced with three additional choices. (1) Move away from her abuser but then remain celibate the rest of her life since divorce is a sin and not recognized by the Church. (2) Get a divorce and remarry anyway, damning her soul for all eternity. (3) Stay with her abuser and hope he doesn't kill her. Some more great choices.

Other religions are less restrictive, but guilt and fear of punishment are still the primary tools employed to keep marriages intact. And the constant railing against prostitution and sins of the flesh seems to imply that the American Family is held together by the thinnest of threads. That is, without the fear of God and his punishments, we would all supposedly jump into bed with the next available person. But that is just not true. Some of us find it possible to love and respect our partners even without Hell snapping at our heels. And we find it difficult to prize fidelity when it is only the result of the fear of heavenly retribution, just as it would not be prized if it only happened because your loved one was locked up in solitary confinement. Morality implies choice, and the only form of fidelity that is truly moral is freely given, not coerced. Freely given, fidelity has great meaning. If it is not freely given, who wants it? Who would cherish grudging, sullen, unwilling, I'm-only-with-you-because-the-church-says-I-have-to-be fidelity?

The Bible also asserts that women alone are responsible for sin by seducing their pure, helpless male counterparts.

". . . with the flattering of her lips she forced him. He goeth after her straightway, as an ox goeth to the slaughter. . . ." (Proverbs 7:21,22)

Forced him, did she? Couldn't he have said no? And don't forget that according to the Bible the entire downfall of humankind in the Garden of Eden was the fault of Eve only. Adam was guiltless. Of course we must then ask why, when he was offered the sinful fruit by his sinful wife, the noble Adam didn't simply refuse. Couldn't he just have said no?

In response to all of the accusations over the ages that women are "temptresses," we must ask in each case, "Couldn't he have said no?" Further, since men have always proclaimed helplessness when confronted with a sultry female, which means that men are the abject slaves of their penises, having no control over their own actions, why have they also insisted that only men should run the world since men are less emotional? There's a serious contradiction here.

The number of sixty-year-old men with twenty-year-old girls on their arms tells a story. And the ease with which the right sized bra cup can convince a politician to change his vote on an important issue, tells a similar, but even more ridiculous story. So we may safely put to sleep, forever, the groundless notion that females are somehow less able to think rationally than are men. It would appear that quite the contrary is true. And all of Christianity's harping about temptresses and wicked women is a pathetic attempt at shifting the blame for stupid human conduct onto the shoulders of attractive women, instead of placing it where it really belongs — underneath those zippers.

In the end, then, it is very clear that Christian teachings about sex, which are stifling and degrading toward women, turn that journey down the aisle into a dreary life sentence for that young, sweet bride. Instead of enjoying one of life's sweetest pleasures, that good Christian girl will spend her life contemplating her shameful body and feeling guilty about her mysterious, evil power over men. She will consider sex and Satan to be synonymous. What a terrible shame.

The Gay Nineties

Referred to as a filthy, immoral practice, homosexuality is one of the biggest taboos in many religions, and it is exhorted against with fury and promises of horrific punishments. This is very strange.

If morality does indeed imply choice, and there is little argument against that proposition, and homosexuality is considered immoral, then those who choose it would of course be immoral. But this brings up an interesting question.

When, exactly, did sexual attraction become a matter of choice? When did we all make this choice? Ask yourself. When did you sit down and decide whether you were going to be attracted to girls or boys? Since it is one of the most important decisions you will ever make in your lifetime, you must surely remember, with crystal clarity, this momentous decision. Well, do you?

If you are like everyone else, you have no such memory. Ask your friends if they have such memories, although it would be a good idea if they were really close friends with open minds, or else tempers might flare. But there will be no dramatic testaments gushed forth about the Big Decision. This is worth thinking about.

No one knows why some of us are homosexual while the rest of us are not. There are negative theories ranging from hormonal imbalance to child abuse to chromosomal damage to The Devil Made Me Do It. We can safely rule out the last offering, but there is no doubt that we simply do not understand why it happens. We just don't know. A great number of us insist that it also doesn't matter.

But I maintain that what we can be certain of is that homosexuality is not a matter of choice, like buying a car. Now *there's* a decision we all remember making. But sexual attraction? No. I remember my own experience clearly. One day I was playing jacks on the sidewalk and wishing that the boys would stop horsing around because they were being a damn nuisance. A few weeks later I was looking at a glamour magazine and trying to figure out how those pretty ladies made their eyelashes look so dark, because I wanted to look the same way. Why? Because I wanted to be attractive to those boys who were no longer a damn nuisance. It was that sudden, that intense and apparently that permanent. I have yet to lose interest. And I had absolutely nothing to do with it. It just happened. Why should I take bows for making such a moral decision? That would be like taking bows for the moral decision to have green eyes or to be double-jointed. These things happen to you. You do not choose them.

The religious moralists, however, would have it another way. One day I was playing jacks on the sidewalk and a few weeks later, supposedly, I locked myself in my bedroom and had a serious talk with myself. "Whom shall I be attracted to," I supposedly asked myself, "girls or boys? Well, let's see. I'll say . . . boys! No! Wait a minute! Girls! No! Wait a minute. Gee, what should I do? Toss a coin?" And then, if I were to make the so-called wrong decision, I would forever be attracted to girls.

Is someone kidding here? Sorry, but it just doesn't work that way. At any age, we have no choice in this matter. We are attracted to what we are attracted to. We might not know why we have certain favorite foods, either, but no amount of lecturing is going to change the fact that our favorite food *appeals*. We might be able to refrain from eating that food, but we cannot eliminate its appeal. What appeals, appeals.

So sexual attraction is not a matter of choice and is therefore not a moral issue. Acting on that attraction, however, is definitely a matter of choice. It is a volitional act. But should it automatically then be considered a moral decision? Volitional? Yes. Moral choice? No. How can it be? If you are hurting no one else by your actions, then morality never enters into it, any more than your choice of colors in your clothing is a moral decision.

A homosexual man may wish, even fervently, that he could find women sexually appealing, since society has for so long pushed this at him. But just as a heterosexual male simply cannot find a man appealing, so it is the other way around. We should realize this instinctively, and deal with it compassionately. But, no, the Bible says that homosexuals "shall surely be put to death," so throughout history we have treated them, inexcusably, like criminals.

Some adults feel sexual attraction for children. However, and this is a *big* however, no one, gay, straight or undetermined, has the right to rape children. Since children by definition cannot provide informed consent to any sexual activity, *all* sexual activity with children is sexual assault. And it cannot be tolerated. If we will not protect our children, there is no one worth protecting. Since the attraction to children is something over which a person has no control, it is therefore not a moral issue. Acting on that attraction, however, is volitional and absolutely a moral choice, since someone will always be hurt by it — *the child*. And here society must step in, using whatever means are necessary to halt the abuse.

So, while society cannot tolerate sexual abuse in any form, homosexual activity between consenting adults hurts no one and should be viewed as the non-threatening activity that it is. We must climb out of the Dark Ages on this issue, and ask ourselves why, if homosexuals hurt us not at all, do we get so mad about it? It's an interesting question.

And the Bible's superstitious, bigoted attitude toward homosexuality must be swept away before we can even begin to approach morality, which is simply a matter of getting along with our fellow humans.

Be Fruitful And Multiply

Most religions have rules regarding sexual behavior, a few of which make some sense in the area of hygiene, but most of which are first, foremost and solely intended to retain control over paternity. Men, who have done all of the writing down of all of the rules of all of the world's religions, and who coincidentally have received all of their revelations from all-male deities, wanted to keep track of whose babies were whose. None of this we're-all-brothers-under-the-skin stuff for them. Which babies are mine? Women of course never had this problem, being one hundred percent certain that the babies that emerged from their bodies were their own. But men could never be sure.

So as the rules of behavior were written down, careful attention was paid to every detail of the sexual activity of women. Virginity in women was valued to a ridiculous extent, far out of proportion to its intrinsic importance in any human community. Women were (and still often are) punished severely for any violation of these sexual strictures. Men, by contrast, allowed themselves (and still often do) to scatter their seed carelessly and constantly, the *double standard* being an ancient human institution.

An important point about these religious sexual laws, especially in the Judeo-Christian tradition, is that while there are harsh penalties for conduct that will lessen the certainty of paternity, the really terrible sexual crimes are not even mentioned in the so-called Ten Commandments. As mentioned briefly in the earlier discussion of the Commandments, rape and child sexual abuse are overlooked. How can this be? How can raping a child not be mentioned in anyone's list of things not to do? Why isn't this heinous abuse of adult power over children deplored loudly and clearly in the Bible?

The Bible goes into tedious detail about how you are unclean after having sex, and a woman is unclean after giving birth (she's unclean longer after delivering a girl than after delivering a boy — figure that one) and adultery and fornication are condemned. But there are no righteous tirades against raping children. Why on earth not?!

The Bible is very confusing about rape. Within your own community, where you care about paternity, rape is condemned. Treated as a man's property, a raped woman is viewed as an affront to the man who owns her, father or husband, and punishments are meted out accordingly. However, raping outside your own community, the enemy for instance, is not only tolerated but encouraged by God.

"Now therefore kill every male among the little ones, and kill every woman that hath known man by lying with him. But all the women children, that have not known a man by lying with him, keep alive for yourselves." (Numbers 31:17,18)

In other words, keep the virgins alive so you can rape them if you choose. This is a strange directive from a loving god. And in Judges 5:28–30, women are doled out as rewards for a good day's battle:

"The mother of Sisera looked out at a window, and cried through the lattice, Why is his chariot so long in coming? why tarry the wheels of his chariots?

"Her wise ladies answered her, yea, she returned answer to herself, Have they not sped? have they not divided the prey; *to every man a damsel or two*; to Sisera a prey of divers colours, a prey of divers colours of needlework, of divers colours of needlework on both sides, meet for the necks of them that take the *spoil?"* (Emphasis added.)

So women, here quaintly referred to as damsels, are considered part of the prey and part of the spoil. The spoils of war have always been an inducement in trying to recruit men to engage in various wars throughout history. And the Bible blandly accepts this despicable conduct, considering it business as usual. Win a battle, rape some virgins. It's all in a day's work. Most people find this extremely offensive.

Although adultery muddles paternity issues, it is a totally nonviolent act. Yet it made the list. It was included in the Ten Commandments. Rape was not. Many people, then, especially rape victims, have wondered how this could have happened. And many would answer that it is because the crime of rape is directed at women almost one hundred percent of the time.

Historically, men in positions of power have cared not at all for the rights of women and children. Women and children were property.

The Bible's silence on abortion, touched on previously, is even more mysterious. If God truly considered it to be an act of murder, as the current Religious Right claims so vociferously, why doesn't the Bible even mention it? You'd think that somewhere in its 1200 or so pages, the Bible would at least broach the subject if it were so important and so wrong. But it does not.

So, we are supposed to believe that, according to the Old Testament God, it was perfectly all right to murder hundreds of thousands of men, women, pregnant women, and children, including infants and sucklings. At the same time we are to believe that, today, it is a heinous crime of murder to remove from a rape victim an embryo with the size, shape and brain capacity of a salamander. There is a loop in this program somewhere. Moreover, in Exodus 21:22, a man found to have caused a miscarriage is punished, but not as if he had killed someone.

The argument that states that since God commanded people to be fruitful and multiply, abortion must be against God's will, is equally tortured reasoning. If you already have given birth to sixteen children and then abort the seventeenth pregnancy, you are supposedly guilty of not being fruitful, which is blatant nonsense.

The issue of abortion is a complicated one, requiring careful solution. Arguably, the most sensible suggestion put forward thus far would recognize, as truly human, any fetus with a fully developed cerebral cortex. That part of the brain, after all, is what separates us from other animals. It actually defines our humanity. And until it comes into existence, the fetus cannot logically be considered a human being, and, therefore, cannot be the object of murder. It seems eminently sensible.

Yet the strident anti-abortionists would have us believe that a zygote, that *one-celled* entity that results from the joining of sperm and ovum, is as human as you are. A zygote, smaller than an amoeba, so small that you need a microscope even to see the thing, supposedly has the same constitutional rights that you do. This is such an extreme position that it is difficult to know where to begin in refuting it. A good place to start, however, might be with miscarriages.

Where are all the funerals? When a Christian woman suffers a tragic miscarriage, why is there not a proper Christian burial? Surely Christians don't believe this *fully human* being should be allowed to slip down a bathroom drainpipe or be thrown out with the hospital garbage? That would be a sacrilege. Such scenarios should arouse the same ire that abortions do among these religious zealots. Remember that according to the Religious Right, these embryos are human beings. As such, they deserve to be named, blessed, placed in a proper coffin, and given a decent, Christian funeral service. Anything less is to deprive this human being of full human status.

This is not a facetious argument. You wouldn't throw your dear old Uncle Henry out with the hospital trash if he died, would you? Of course not. And people go to incredible lengths to retrieve the mortal remains of their dearly beloved sons and daughters killed in action during wartime, don't they? Their only purpose in seeking that retrieval is to provide a decent burial. So the same respect should be shown these so-called fully human embryos. If you must fish something messy from a bathroom bowl, so be it. This is a human being you're talking about here, so a funeral is called for. It would necessarily be difficult to put an age on the tombstone. The numeral "0" might be appropriate.

There is no way to avoid the preceding unpleasantness if fully human status is granted to all embryos. This same line of reasoning will carry you forward inexorably, inevitably, until you reach the point so dramatically demonstrated once on the *Geraldo* show. Two Catholic priests sat there and calmly announced that since doctors who perform abortions are murderers, the doctors themselves should be put to death for their capital crimes. Not just the doctors, but their receptionists also should be put to death. And the nurses. And the doctors' wives. And the truck drivers who deliver supplies to the doctors. This is a true story.

Most of us would say that those priests were looney-tunes. But if you follow the Catholic Church's position on abortion to its logical conclusion, those priests were correct in their positions. You cannot have it both ways. Either an embryo is a human being or it is not. Take your pick. Having chosen, you must then follow through on your position or lose all credibility. The priests were right. It is the Catholic Church that is wrong for teaching and encouraging such extremism.

And unless and until all of the world's millions of children are loved and cared for, the whole issue seems moot anyway. Every child should have the right to be born to a mother who wants it. The Pope's constant rantings about the evils of birth control, and therefore condoms, have no place in a world bulging at the seams with over five billion people, and with millions of starving (unplanned) children.

There is a world filled with brocaded robes and strange looking hats; with cavernous, hushed rooms, adorned with priceless art work and redolent with costly incense; and 24-karat-gold crucifixes caressed by the bejeweled hands of self-proclaimed, lifelong celibates. Then there is the real world. Most of us live in that real world, not in the Vatican, and it is time that the Vatican either woke up to that fact or withdrew into its medieval cocoon and left the rest of us alone.

To preach *only* abstinence is to pretend that sex is not part of our humanity. The Church's own clergy can't even practice abstinence, as thousands of priest-raped children will tell you.

Adding insult to injury is the fact that the Vatican possesses literally billions of dollars in assets in its art collection, its portfolio of stocks and bonds, and its vast real estate holdings. Those billions could feed a tremendous number of hungry children, as well as providing urgently needed medical care. So why isn't it being done?

For the Vatican to cling to its billions, knowing full well how many thousands of children die of starvation every single day, and knowing also that many of those children are Catholic, is the epitome of hypocrisy and greed. Catholic charities are often given (justified) credit for raising money to help the needy, but these are private citizens. I seriously doubt that any Pope has ever baked a cake for a cake-sale to help the poor. But since he is insisting on maximum birth rates, he, of all people, should pitch in, sell some jewelry and paintings, and help to end some of the horrific suffering of the world's children. Refusing to do so puts the Church in a truly ignoble position. While insisting, on pain of eternal damnation, that its members must have babies whether they can afford to feed them or not, it then refuses to help feed those very babies. This is indefensible.

Some argue that even if the Vatican sold *all* of its treasures, it would not end world hunger. So? A cake-sale won't end world hunger, either. Yet millions of caring people organize and patronize such activities in an effort, at least, to help. A world filled with starving children (many of them Catholic) and a Vatican brimming with untold riches, should not coexist in a sane world.

So, perhaps the Bishop of Rome should put his own house in order before launching into any further sermons about the evils of birth control and abortion. He should rid his Catholic clergy of all of its many, disgusting child-molesters, and he should then see to it that there is not one single Catholic child, anywhere on Earth, going to bed hungry. Physician, heal thyself.

What makes all this so ironic is that the Bible takes no stand on the abortion issue at all. You're on your own. It's time we all cooled off about this thing, and, instead of screaming slogans at each other, approached the problem with some compassion and intelligence. And let's leave religion in the churches where it belongs.

6

The Messiah

He comes into the world God knows how, walks on the water, gets out of his grave and goes up off the Hill of Howth. What drivel is this?

James Joyce, *Stephen Hero*

Just whether or not Jesus was an actual, historical figure is the subject of much scholarly debate. St. Paul, who was the real founder of the religion known as Christianity, barely discussed Jesus as a person, and made no references to his family. Jesus must remain a puzzle, historically speaking. He may have existed, and then again he may not have.

Many scholars believe that if you were to take as many Old Testament passages as you could find that could be construed as referring to a Messiah who would be arriving someday to be the Savior of the Jews, and if you then pasted all those passages together and tried to invent a person who would match the descriptions in them, you would end up with Jesus. The Jesus of the New Testament, many claim, was simply a product of wish-fulfillment, or, in this case, prophecy-fulfillment. The Old Testament said such a person should be arriving, and so a lot of people decided that he had arrived.

Ironically, most of the Jews, who claimed the Bible as their own originally, chose not to believe that the Messiah had arrived. But Christianity had been born, largely due to the efforts of St. Paul, and it is still with us today. In a big way.

But let's set aside these scholarly differences and grant, for the sake of discussion, the fact that Jesus really lived as Christians say he did and really died as they say he did. If you read the biblical narratives relating those events, you are still going to be left with many troubling, unanswered questions. The four main gospels in the New Testament unfortunately do not agree with each other in many respects. But let's also set aside these difficulties, and look at the overall account of the birth of Jesus.

For Unto Us A Child Is Born

The reason so many Christmas trees are topped with an angel is that it represents the angel who came to Earth to announce the birth of Jesus to some shepherds in the fields nearby. Why shepherds? That's a very good question, but so far no reasonable answer has ever been offered. It would have made much more sense to announce this special birth to all of the world leaders, rather than to a handful of shepherds.

Nevertheless, if local shepherds were notified of the history-making birth taking place in a nearby stable, whatever became of those shepherds? If an angel appeared to *you* one night, surely it would be a major event in your life, indelibly etched into your memory. It would easily take up more than one page in your diary. So why didn't those shepherds race to the stable, observe the Blessed Babe, and then remain in attendance for the rest of their natural lives? Wouldn't you stick close by someone whose birth had been announced to you by an *angel?*

But the Bible records no such behavior. The shepherds went to the stable, acknowledged the Savior of the World, and then calmly went back to their sheep-tending, never to be heard from again. Strange, indeed.

Similarly, the Three Wise Men we have heard so much about made their treks to the stable from far-off lands, and offered gifts to the newborn Savior of the World. Then, they also just went back home where they came from, never to be heard from again. This is beyond strange.

Even today, people are willing to sell all of their worldly goods, follow some guru up to the top of some mountain, and there await the End of the World. It happens. And these people do it all without any angels prompting their bizarre behavior. So how could the shepherds and the Wise Men have reacted with such nonchalance after acknowledging what was to them the real, honest-to-goodness Savior of the World? It doesn't make sense.

The way the Wise Men found this much-visited stable is even more suspect. The so-called Star of Bethlehem supposedly guided these men to the Babe in the Manger. But the most cursory introduction to astronomy will inform you that in order for a star to guide you to a specific town, let alone a specific building, it would have to be no higher than a thousand feet in the air. Any higher and you will be guided only to a general area, just as the North Star can guide you generally northward. But if the Star of Bethlehem did indeed shine over that famous stable, it had to be so low in the Earth's atmosphere that it could not possibly have been a star or a comet. And meteors don't stand still long enough to guide anyone anywhere. The Star of Bethlehem can only be a fictional ornament, invented by very unsophisticated writers.

Many of us, believers as well as nonbelievers, tend to get so caught up in the ideological details of the religions we're bickering about, that we often overlook the actual, physical premises of those very religions. The nitty-gritty of the Christian nativity story too often is glossed over as True Believers focus instead on the rapturous concept of eternal salvation. The Babe in the Manger scene, for example, brings lumps to the throats of millions. And "Away In A Manger" is melodically one of the prettiest carols ever written. But before you can have a Babe in the Manger, you first must have a Babe.

The Bible goes to incredible lengths to assure us that Mary's pregnancy was the result of some magical joining with the Holy Ghost, one-third of the so-called Triune God. In this way her conception is removed from any possible taint of carnal knowledge. Mary supposedly gave birth while still a virgin.

This same Bible, however, does not go to such lengths in describing just how the heavenly babe was born. In a stable, they say, but no other details are provided. We must assume, therefore, in the absence of biblical evidence to the contrary, that a normal, human childbirth took place in that stable. One would hope that Mary was spared a long labor and a breech birth. But let's not forget that a stable is for animals and a manger is a trough used to feed animals.

It is clear that this unlikely setting for the birth of the world's savior was intended to convey a humble birth, something we all supposedly can identify with. However, a stable means animals, animals mean dung, and dung means tremendous amounts of bacteria and pungent, offensive odors. Fleas and ticks also spring to mind. This is not a pretty picture.

How Mary escaped death from "childbed fever" is a mystery. (Many of our not-so-remote female ancestors died from such a cause, which was really nothing more than assaulting a newly vulnerable body with more bacterial infection than it could handle. The famous nineteenth-century doctor, Ignaz Semmelweis [1818–1865] drove himself crazy trying to convince his colleagues at least to wash their hands before delivering babies, but all to no avail. Dirty hands delivered, thousands upon thousands of women died, and all for a lack of soap-and-water technology. But that's another story.)

Christians might argue that since this was the Son of God being born here, such mundane details did not apply. However, that argument will eliminate Jesus as ever having been *human*, a position no Christian is willing to concede. So we'll have to count Mary just plain lucky.

The most popular story of the birth of Jesus is recorded in Luke (Chapter 2). It is read and heard by millions every year, and it appears on television in cartoons and so-called documentaries. Most notable about this account are the verses that are invariably left out during any reading of these passages. Luke's nativity story ends, almost always, with the shepherds praising God. But if you read the next four verses, you will hear the rest of the story. It is as follows:

When the Baby Jesus was eight days old they sliced off the very tip of his penis with a knife. And when Mary's "purification" was completed she and Joseph took the baby to Jerusalem to present him to the Lord, since "Every male that openeth the womb shall be called holy to the Lord." After that they killed two young pigeons, or two turtledoves, take your pick, and offered them as sacrifices to God.

All of that is crammed into four short verses, and those verses directly follow the description of the celebrating shepherds. So why are they conscientiously avoided during Christmas-time Bible readings? It's simple. Those four verses take the lump out of your throat in a hurry. The idea that Mary was unclean just because she gave birth, and was in need of purification rites, is embarrassingly primitive and without any medical basis whatsoever. It is bald superstition. Further, the idea that only male first-born children were considered holy is a ringing endorsement of male chauvinism, and an insult to all women and girls. The idea that only first-born children were considered holy is an insult to ninety-nine percent of the human race. And finally, sacrificing birds to a god is about as primitive as it is possible to be. We're talking a Stone Age mentality here. And *that* is why the Luke nativity story is always cut short.

Christian artwork is resplendent with portraits displaying Jesus being held against Mary's breast. Halos abound and Mary smiles down beatifically at the holy babe at her breast. The imagery is unmistakable. Supposedly we are to infer something other-worldly about the straightforward process of lactation. Why? Perhaps Mary had chafing problems or suffered periods of insufficient milk production. These are very real, very common, very human problems. If Mary nursed Jesus, she would have been subject to the same universal nursing problems that all women have been subject to since the dawn of history.

Likewise, if Jesus was at one time a real baby, he had to have had his diapers changed regularly. Did he ever suffer from diaper rash? Did he ever have colic? Was he difficult to toilet train? Did he cry while he was teething?

When anyone tries to ask these questions about what Christians insist was a natural, mother-child relationship between Mary and Jesus, Christians balk. Such questions seem totally inappropriate when directed at a supposedly omnipotent god. But in balking, Christians are trying to have it both ways. They insist that Jesus underwent the total *human* experience, in addition to being a god. But then they turn around and deny that Jesus ever experienced most human conditions. This doesn't work. They want it both ways, but they may not have it both ways.

True Believers often point out that out since Jesus was the supposed Son of God, he would have been a perfect human being, so none of the various human maladies would ever have accosted him. But if you're perfect, you're not human. You must choose one or the other. And if Jesus was going to be a *perfect* human being, why did Mary have to go through a human, physical pregnancy? Why didn't Jesus just descend, fully grown, from a cloud?

And, getting down to reality, there is simply no such thing as a perfect dirty diaper. Babies are babies and diapers are diapers. The god-thing doesn't work here.

It seems that most Christians can't quite make up their minds about Jesus' supposed true nature. Their indecisiveness in this matter, however, does not prevent us from asking incisive questions. He is their god and they must explain him. The burden of proof is theirs.

So, the questions, rightly, must continue. When Jesus was a baby and learning to walk, did he stumble and fall like all other human babies? Did he ever scratch an itch? Or sneeze? Or have indigestion? Or have a head cold? Did he have any adolescent acne? Did he urinate and defecate like all other males? Did he have to comb his hair? Did he ever have a toothache? Did he dream while he slept? Did he snore? Did he ever feel sexual arousal? Did he ever have a belly laugh over a good joke?

Obviously the questions could go on almost indefinitely. And these questions make Jesus seem less and less god-like, and more and more human, which is why most Christians shy away from considering them. But if they insist on Jesus' full humanity as well as his god status, they must grapple with such issues as dandruff, athlete's foot and hay fever. If this thought brings a smile to your lips, ask yourself why. What is funny about mundane human conditions?

The humor in the situation lies in the image of an eternal, all-powerful god scratching at a mosquito bite. It just doesn't work. It is difficult enough for many of us to imagine the concept of a god of any kind, even one that is ephemeral, unknowable, and floating in space somewhere. But this being known as Jesus, plodding around ancient Palestine in his sandals, simply cannot be considered to have been simultaneously an eternally perfect god-being. It just doesn't fly, no matter how many halos you paint into your artists' renditions of that being.

By definition, a god is not a man and vice versa. If Christians want to revere Jesus as a great teacher among humans, fine. If they want to consider him as a god, they are certainly free to do so. But rationalists cannot understand how any intelligent, logically-minded adult can reconcile heavenly holiness with a hangnail.

Miracle On Main Street

Very few of us have ever seen a miracle, although we use the word all the time. "The doctors said he probably wouldn't live, but look at him now! It's a miracle!" That word gets bandied about carelessly, and has become almost synonymous with surprising event. But it doesn't mean surprising event. It means that something has happened that cannot be explained by any natural means and, therefore, must be of *super*-natural origin. It's your basic walking on water.

The Jesus of the New Testament performed, they say, many miracles. Since he was supposedly a god, there is nothing particularly strange about that. What is strange, however, is the type of miracles he performed. Walking on water, for example, as Jesus supposedly did (Matthew 14:26) would be considered a real feat by anyone. But what value did such a performance have? Was anyone really helped by Jesus' supposed walking on the water? Was any human suffering alleviated by this stunt? Why would a god waste something as precious as a miracle just to show off to his friends? The lame explanation that Jesus was trying to instill faith in his disciples carries no weight whatsoever in a world filled with human suffering.

Even more silly is Jesus' turning water into wine for a wedding celebration. (John 2:1–11) Now there's a worthy cause, making sure that a bunch of drunks have enough wine at a wedding. The miracle apparently was performed on six waterpots containing two or three "firkins" of water apiece. After the wedding guests were all sloshy and happy, this magnanimous, compassionate, first miracle (Jesus' opening act, as it were) was said to have "manifested forth his glory." Can anyone claim, without laughing, that booze could ever be considered even marginally important, let alone worthy of the invoking of a miracle? The tragedy of alcoholism aside, booze is booze. To try to impart to it some symbolic importance in world affairs is about as silly as it gets. In fact, this water-into-wine business is enough, all by itself, to destroy the Bible's credibility. The world has always needed more compassion, more forgiveness and more humor. It has *never* needed more booze.

The allegedly illustrious career of Jesus goes on to include a feeding miracle. On one occasion (Matthew 14:16–21) he managed to make two fish and five loaves of bread feed over five thousand people. Talk about stretching leftovers. (There is no explanation offered, in the description of this feeding miracle, as to how these thousands of people, all gathered to hear Jesus' words, could have heard anything spoken at all. This was, remember, before microphones had been invented. Try to imagine making your voice heard to over five thousand people, out in the open air, with no P.A. system. It's impossible.)

In addition to feeding *some* people with this ostentatious proffer of miracle food, while many thousands of people in other parts of the world were at that moment dying of starvation, Jesus supposedly also performed healings. Of course he only healed a few here and a few there. There was no worldwide elimination of, say, malaria, or leprosy. Actually there was nothing in these healings at all that benefited humankind. Eliminating all disease, altogether, would have been a nifty miracle, one certainly worthy of the name, and one that would attract, literally, a world full of followers. But instead this all-powerful, eternal god chose to limit his healing to a handful of people in one tiny pocket of civilization.

Likewise, Jesus chose to resurrect from the dead precious few. Why? Resurrecting the dead, if you did it often enough, would soon convince the entire world, not just twelve devoted disciples, that you were powerful and that you meant business. In addition, just think of the overwhelming happiness you would bring to those who had lost dearly loved family members. Why not spread the joy around? With the power over life and death at your fingertips, why use it so sparingly? Once again, it smacks of showing off.

Mark 5:1–13 relates an incredible story wherein Jesus casts out the "devils" from an unfortunate man. He then causes the devils to enter, instead, a herd of swine, and the swine, thus bedeviled, race over a cliff, fall into the sea and drown. Fundamentalists would have us believe that this is a true story. That tells us a lot about fundamentalists. Belief in demons and fairies and goblins and dragons ended, for most people, ages ago, and is remembered only in some of our Fairy Tales. Such primeval superstitions should be left behind, in our colorful past, where they belong.

But all in all, the track record for the Savior of the World, with regard to miracles, is spotty at best and most un-godly. If you're going to heal the sick, heal *all* the sick. If you're going to raise the dead, raise *all* the dead. If you're going to walk on water, save it for when you're alone. Don't do it to show off in front of your friends — not in a world full of people struggling with disease, wars, and starvation.

Because these supposed miracles are so remote in time, many people refuse to look at them the same way they would look at such alleged miracles today. Aside from the gullible individuals who, once or twice every year, go racing off somewhere to visit statues of the Virgin Mary to view her tears or something, most people today would reject, out of hand, any claims of miracles that were anywhere near as bizarre as those mentioned in the New Testament. But there is no reason for viewing ancient miracles any differently than you would modern miracles. The laws of nature have not changed in two thousand years. Up is still up. Gravity still works. Water runs downhill, and payday is often on a Friday. There are very few things new under the sun.

But people generally don't believe in miracles that happen on their own turf. That's because they are so familiar with their own turf. There's nothing mystical about the weeds growing in your own backyard. This was also true in Jesus' day. Jesus' hometown crowd didn't buy his act, so to speak. Then as now, no one can believe in a miracle on Main Street.

Who would believe, for example, someone's claim that he walked on the water under the Brooklyn Bridge? Would anyone really believe that? Would anyone understand it if they did believe it? If the water-walking, the demons and the dead-body-resurrecting seem totally implausible today, they were equally implausible two thousand years ago.

It may be a lovely fantasy, to think about a benevolent god who can work miracles for us. We can all probably think of exactly what we'd ask for if such a thing were true. But it's hard to imagine anyone, anywhere, at any time, asking an all-powerful god to spring for a half dozen jugs of wine.

Separate Checks, Please

The Last Supper as described in the New Testament was the occasion where Jesus shared his final Jewish Passover meal with his twelve disciples. But he added a new wrinkle. In anticipation of his imminent, sacrificial death, he instructed his followers to eat the bread he had just blessed, saying, "Take, eat; this is my body." (Matthew 26:26) Then he gave them a cup of wine saying, "Drink ye all of it; For this is my blood. . . ." Kind of takes away the appetite.

Many primitive, sacrificing societies believed that if you ate the flesh and drank the blood of a human being recently endowed, by their own magical rites, with god-like attributes, that those very attributes would somehow be transferred to those doing the eating and drinking. Similarly, many believed that if you were at war with a powerful adversary, and you managed to capture, kill and eat one or more of them, you would somehow acquire your adversary's power. In some groups fingers were considered a bit of a treat. Yuck.

These matters are sickeningly difficult to discuss. But in light of the startling similarities between these cannibalistic beliefs and Jesus' Last Supper, they must be considered. The idea of becoming part of, or "communing" with a god, by eating him or his representation on Earth, makes almost all of us grimace as our stomachs turn. Yet this is precisely what modern Christians are acting out every time they celebrate Communion in their church services. Communion is symbolic cannibalism, nothing more and nothing less.

As if the institution of this offensive ritual did not provide enough drama at this Last Supper, Jesus also announced that one of his twelve disciples, sitting there with him, would soon betray him. Judas was the treacherous disciple who, for a sum of money, was going to kiss Jesus on the cheek in front of a "great multitude" that included "chief priests" and "elders." (Matthew 26:47) The kiss would identify the person to be arrested and ultimately put to death.

Undoubtedly this announcement of betrayal dispelled any feeling of camaraderie at the supper. And what followed immediately after was certainly unpleasant. What happened was this. After supper, Jesus went to a place called Gethsemane to pray, while his disciples waited a short distance away. Jesus prayed to his father, asking if perhaps his upcoming death could be avoided. Apparently the answer was no.

Then, when Jesus had finished praying, Judas and his multitude approached with "swords and staves." The infamous kiss of betrayal was planted on Jesus' cheek, and he was taken away. His disciples fled in all directions. The Jewish scribes and elders held a hearing wherein they decided that Jesus was guilty of blasphemy (to speak irreverently of God or sacred things). Meanwhile, one of the disciples, Peter, three times denied that he had ever even *known* Jesus.

Now instead of killing Jesus themselves, the elders took him to the Roman procurator, or governor, Pontius Pilate, and asked *him* to kill Jesus. Pilate, understandably confused, asked, "Why?" The Jews complained that Jesus was calling himself a god, which should be considered treason. Reluctantly, Pilate ordered that Jesus be whipped and then crucified. He was. And he died.

A lot of what transpires in this story is highly suspect. The betrayal kiss is a real puzzle since those very priests and elders who were supposed to be tipped off as to whom to arrest, saw Jesus on a regular basis and knew him quite well. There was no need for a line-up here. It makes no sense at all, unless you are trying to force the Jesus character of the New Testament to fit into the mold created by prophecies in the Old Testament.

We are reminded that many scholars believe Jesus, as a person, never existed. Rather, he was a personage manufactured out of Old Testament prophecies. And in the case of Judas' totally unnecessary, finger-pointing kiss of death, we see such tortuous manufacturing. In the Old Testament, Psalms 41:9 states, "Yea, mine own familiar friend, in whom I trusted, which did eat of my bread, hath lifted up his heel against me." See how it works?

Just why Jesus would pray to be spared a death that defined his only reason for being is another puzzle. What sense does that make? And whom was he praying *to*? His father, they say, but then they also say there is only one god here, the Triune God, the Father, Son and Holy Ghost. All one god. So Jesus must have been praying, in part, to himself. But his asking to be freed of his sole obligation here on Earth is inexplicable.

And why did all his disciples run away? Why would they desert Jesus at the very moment that he was preparing to fulfill his destiny? Why have disciples at all then? Or, perhaps a better question, why not get better disciples? This puzzle also defies reason.

Turning Jesus over to the Roman procurator, however, is the most unlikely, unbelievable part of this whole story. At the time, Rome had just emerged from decades of the unarguably brilliant leadership of Augustus, only to be plunged into the chaos of Tiberius' rule, followed by the rule of the sadistic, twisted Caligula. (He was ultimately assassinated by his own Praetorian Guard.) The last thing Rome cared about was an upstart Jew claiming to be the Son of God.

So the idea that the Roman powers-that-be would give a rap, one way or another, about Jesus, is simply not credible. And no Roman procurator, Pontius Pilate included, was ever coerced into doing anything against his will by a rowdy crowd. No way. Pilate did what he pleased, concerned only with approval from the hierarchy, and crucifying some unknown Jew because he was squabbling with his own religious leaders would never have crossed his mind.

Pontius Pilate was plucked from the pages of history by the gospel writers, who did their writing about a half century after the supposed events they were describing, because Pilate was procurator during the time frame that fit in with their story. There is no other explanation for the gospel writers' account of a Roman procurator getting involved with the Jewish community's religious squabbles.

He Is Risen?

Every Bible critic from the earliest to the most recent, has pointed out the many inconsistencies in the various gospel accounts of the resurrection of Jesus. John E. Remsberg in his book *The Christ* (originally published in 1909), lists over twenty-five gospel discrepancies regarding the resurrection alone. He also lists over six hundred discrepancies overall in the gospels. These all must be explained, but so far no one has been able to do so.

To begin with, it would be reasonable to expect that in the most important book ever written, a book inspired by The One True Omnipotent God, there would be no errors whatsoever. That would seem to be a given. Yet the Bible is so riddled with contradictions that it is often impossible to tell a coherent Bible story by using only biblical texts, and without adding your own explanatory footnotes.

To illustrate just how confusing the gospels are regarding the resurrection of Jesus, I tried to write a simple story of what happened on that first Easter Day, using only the gospels as sources. This is what I came up with:

When the sun had risen or when it was still dark, we're not sure which, Mary Magdalene and the other Mary, or Mary Magdalene, the mother of James, and Salome, or Mary

Magdalene, Joanna, Mary the mother of James and some other women, or just Mary Magdalene, we're not sure who, went to visit Jesus' tomb. They came to bring spices to anoint the body, or the body had already been spiced and they just came to take a look, we're not sure which. When they (she) arrived they encountered one angel sitting on the stone, or one young man sitting inside the tomb on the right, or two men standing inside, or two angels, each sitting on one end of the funeral bed, we're not sure which.

The messengers either told the women not to be afraid, since Jesus had risen from the dead, or they asked one woman why she was crying, we're not sure which. The women either told no one about it, or they told all eleven of Jesus' disciples about it, we're not sure which. Mary, Jesus' mother, first saw her resurrected son before she went to see the disciples, or after, we're not sure which. When Mary returned from the tomb, she either knew Jesus had been resurrected, or she did not know he had been resurrected, we're not sure which. Jesus could be touched after his resurrection, or he could not be touched after his resurrection, we're not sure which.

After appearing to the women, Jesus next appeared either to his eleven disciples, or to two disciples in the country, or to two disciples in Emmaus, or to ten disciples, or to Peter and then to Jesus' *twelve* disciples, we're not sure which. Of course by this time Judas was dead so that there could only be eleven disciples, unless they had gained one since the crucifixion, in which case he was never named or referred to in any way. (Judas died either by falling down and having his "bowels gush out" or by hanging himself, we're not sure which.)

After his resurrection, Jesus first appeared to his disciples on a mountain in Galilee, or in Emmaus, or in Jerusalem (seventy-five or so miles from Galilee), we're not sure which. The disciples marched (must have been "quick-time") back and forth between Jerusalem and Galilee, walking a hundred and fifty miles in one day.

Jesus ascended into Heaven the same day that he rose from the dead, or he stayed on Earth for at least eight days more, or for at least forty days more, we're not sure which. Or he may possibly not have ascended at all, since Matthew and John make no mention of this astonishing event. If he did ascend, he did it from near Jerusalem, or from Bethany, or from the Mount of Olives, we're not sure which.

I think it's safe to say that the above account is muddled at best, and ridiculous at worst. Thus far, though, no one has been able to write a more coherent account, including Christians who have challenged me on this point. The only way they can make sense of this chaotic chronicle is to add their own explanations, such as, "We can probably assume. . . ." and, "It seems to be implied. . . ." and, "What probably happened was. . . ." In other words, they must rewrite the Bible.

For example, one gospel states that Judas hanged himself after betraying Jesus, while another gospel states that he fell and had his bowels gush out, obviously contradictory accounts. Yet one Christian apologist actually suggested, seriously, that Judas could easily have hanged himself and *then* fallen from the tree and had his bowels gush out, thus eliminating the contradiction. But for one of the gospel writers to describe Judas' death without mentioning the hanging part, would be like writing a biography of John F. Kennedy without mentioning how he died. Yet these are the extremes that Christians must go to in order to try to reconcile that which is irreconcilable.

However, in adding their own footnotes to the Bible, Christians thus forfeit any claims to biblical inerrancy. They are turning the Bible into a do-it-yourself book, subject to speculation, assumption and wildly divergent interpretations. This can only lead to religious chaos, and this is precisely what we have today.

Look in the Yellow Pages of any telephone directory in a medium- to large-sized city, and check the listings for "Churches, Christian." You will find page after page of different denominations, all claiming to be Christian, but all teaching different, contradictory things. (The "sin" of birth control is a most prominent, bitterly controversial example.) This is what you'd expect if Christianity were based on ancient, unreliable, non-divinely inspired documents. It is not what you'd expect if Christianity were based on documents inspired by an omnipotent god who furnished these accounts to specially selected servants of that god. In that case you would rightly expect perfection. But the Bible doesn't even come close.

How did this come to be? Shouldn't the most important book ever written, telling The Greatest Story Ever Told, be the epitome of eloquence and comprehensibility? Shouldn't it ring out with articulate clarity?

Consider this analogy. Let's say you had an urgent message for all of humankind. How would you try to convey it? Would you go up on the Internet and do your best on the Worldwide Web? Or would you scribble your message on a piece of paper, put it in a corked bottle, toss it into the ocean, and then hope someone finds it? Amazingly, this latter option was the one exercised by God in deciding how to spread the message of his son, Jesus.

To be sure, there was no Internet in Jesus' day. But God had something far more effective than any computer network ever designed. He had *supernatural* powers at his beck and call, and there is no limit to the number of possible means he could have employed in getting his Message to humans. He could have sent legions of angels, for example, to every country on Earth, informing everyone, in their own languages, of Jesus' sacrificial death and subsequent resurrection. So why didn't he?

Doing it the way he did, God made his supposedly Divine Message subject to the vagaries of translation errors, interpolations and self-serving censorship, all of which exist in today's Bible.

There is also a real problem with the timing of Jesus' supposed death and resurrection. It happened long after countless millions had already lived and died, and poses some serious theological problems. These are dealt with elsewhere. (See "The One True God.")

But even at the exact point in history that Jesus supposedly fulfilled his earthly mission, most of the world was not allowed to hear about it. God entrusted his all-important Message, intended for the entire world, only to a tiny handful of men, who all lived in the same place, and who had no way of communicating this news to anyone beyond walking distance. Why?

Christians take pious pride in the so-called Great Commission, "Go, ye, therefore, and teach all nations, baptizing them. . . ." And today they take that commandment quite seriously, which is why those people keep ringing your doorbell and telling you how to be saved *correctly*. But at the time that commandment was given, in the first half of the first century, how could all nations have been notified? That original handful of evangelists knew nothing of the world beyond the cultures huddled around the Mediterranean. They didn't even know the Americas existed, for example, let alone how to get there. And the story of Jesus' life wasn't even put into writing until forty to ninety years after the events in question. This means that in the interim, the accounts of those all-important events were passed on only by word of mouth.

Did you ever play that game, "Telephone," when you were a child? A group of children sits on the floor, in a circle, and one child thinks up a message. She then whispers this message to the child on her right, who then whispers it to *his* right, and so on, until the message finally gets back to the child who thought it up. The final whispered message is never the same as the original version. Usually the author of the message will giggle with glee to hear how distorted the message has become. Without any trickery intended, since the point of the game is to get the message right, distortions still occur. And we're talking here about only seven or eight kids and one or two minutes of time.

This same game is one of your more wholesome adult party games. Sitting on the floor, of course, is optional, but the whispering is not. And in the adult version, the original message is two, short sentences, and is written on a piece of paper. The very last message-bearer does not whisper, but rather makes his announcement out loud, while everyone else hovers around the original, written message. The two messages never match.

Everyone, usually, is startled at this. And then begins the merry fun of trying to figure out who "screwed up" first. Even without cocktails that might confuse things a bit, that two-sentence message never makes it around the room intact. People are always surprised by this fact, and repeat performances are usually demanded, with stern admonitions to get it right this time. But they never do.

The obvious point here is that the Christian message had decades of only word-of-mouth transmission, almost guaranteeing distortions and "screw-ups." Since then, there have been twenty centuries and scores of intermediaries to distort the written word. And distorted it became. It took over fifteen centuries for the Message to reach South America, and when it got there it was accompanied by The Inquisition, a most ugly calling card. (And a part of history the Catholic Church would like to ignore, but may not.) After sixteen centuries, Europeans were still killing each other over doctrinal disputes about Jesus, in the Thirty Years' War, the French massacre of the Huguenots, and so on.

It is difficult to imagine a more inefficient means of spreading the story of Christianity than the one that was used. To this day, large sections of the world know nothing of Christianity, and are perfectly content without it. And to make a guessing game out of the Bible, considering its purported importance, is to posit a guess-what-I'm-saying! prankster of a god. The Bible is an enigma where no enigma should exist.

None of this makes any sense unless Christianity, like all other religions, is just a human creation, designed to try to explain the mysteries of existence. If the Bible were truly the word of God, it should be easily understood by every human on Earth. Every country on Earth should be joining hands in the worship of our One True God. But does this sound like a description of the world today? Does it sound like the world at any point in history?

If not, then the gospels, the "Good News," cannot have originated with an all-powerful, all-wise deity. And the "risen" Jesus will have to join the ranks of the "risen" Osiris, the "risen" Mithra, the "risen" Tammuz, and many more pre-Christian savior-gods who died and then rose from the dead.

So then, when someone jubilantly, or rapturously, asks you to celebrate the fact that the Savior of the world rose from the dead, you must ask, "But which one?"

Jesus And Jehovah

Many Christians delicately try to separate their "gentle" Jesus of the New Testament from the wrathful Jehovah of the Old Testament. But it can't be done. Make no mistake about it, they are one and the same god.

Christians proudly and definitively assert that Jesus was God incarnate. That is, God became flesh in the form of a human being. That human being was Jesus. For Christians, Jehovah himself descended to Earth as Jesus Christ.

Christianity is based upon the concept of the One True God being the Triune God (Father, Son and Holy Ghost) and if that concept is challenged then Christianity is challenged. There is only one god, according to Christians, and even though this god consists of three different personages, it is still only one god. (See

"The One-Sided Triangle.") The Holy Trinity is the bedrock of Christianity.

The concept of a Triune God, three personages within one being, is very difficult to understand or explain. (Or believe.) Perhaps the best analogy would be that of a three-headed dragon. It would be a single being, but it would possess three separate personalities. A Triune God, and a three-headed dragon. Both single beings. Both with three distinct personages. And both equally likely to exist.

Even though it's easy to understand why Christians would like to distance themselves, as well as their gentle Jesus, from the scores of massacres and slaughters found in the Old Testament, it simply can't be done. It's a package deal. If you accept the New Testament you must accept the Old Testament. Why? Because the New Testament spends a great deal of time explaining how the actions of Jesus are fulfilling Old Testament prophesies.

The Old Testament is the foundation for the New Testament, and without it, much of the New Testament just doesn't make any sense. For example, the very first verse of the first chapter of the first book of the New Testament purports to trace the genealogy of Jesus back to the Abraham of the Old Testament. Kind of hard to ignore that one.

And almost every significant act of Jesus as recorded in the New Testament is accompanied by an Old Testament reference, and pointed to as fulfilling those Old Testament prophesies. From Jesus' baptism to his betrayal by Judas, the Old Testament is constantly referred to as having predicted those very things. The Old Testament book of Isaiah, particularly, is quoted repeatedly in the New Testament.

The Jewish Bible contains none of the New Testament books at all. So they don't have any link-up problems to contend with. Their Bible ends before Jesus is even born, so they can, quite legitimately, just ignore the New Testament. But it doesn't work the other way around.

The two books, the Old Testament and the New Testament, are inseparable if you believe the Jesus story. To deny the Old Testament is to deny Jesus. And, supposedly, the three personages in the Holy Trinity are only one being. With this in mind, the biblical slaughters in the Old Testament take on a whole new light. When God decided to kill all those people in the Old Testament, Jesus was part of that decision-making process. (No one knows if they voted or what, but at least with three personages you'll always have a tie-breaker.) The point, though, is that there is no getting around the fact that the God who rained terror and death down onto his own creations, over and over, was in fact Jesus.

The Amalekite massacre, where Saul was ordered to "Slay both man and woman, infant and suckling. . . ." (1 Samuel 15:3) was ordered by Jesus. When the entire world was flooded and everyone in it was killed, except for a small handful of people, that global slaughter was ordered by Jesus. The list of slaughters referred to earlier, can all be, in fact must all be, laid at the door of Jesus. God-The-Father and God-The-Holy Ghost were of course involved, but no more so than God-The-Son (Jesus). Being one-third of the so-called Holy Trinity, Jesus was one-third responsible for all of the Old Testament killings. It's difficult to see how any Christian could refute that.

When you look at it that way, Jesus is suddenly illuminated

with a most unflattering spotlight. It is difficult, even for nonbelievers, to picture Jesus participating in decisions to kill hundreds of thousands of people. We have all been conditioned to think of Jesus as a wise, kind, teacher and healer. A gentle man. Well, that gentleman was in agreement with the order that the Samaritans were to "fall by the sword: their infants shall be dashed in pieces, and their women with child shall be ripped up." (Hosea 13:16)

Christians don't like to think about these things. Actually, nonbelievers don't like to think about them either, but for different reasons. For Christians, it's an embarrassing reminder that their gentle Jesus killed wantonly. For nonbelievers, it is simply cruel, repulsive and sickening.

Jesus' own utterances are often ticklishly embarrassing. "Think not that I am come to send peace on earth: I came not to send peace, but a sword." (Matthew 10:34) "But those mine enemies, which would not that I should reign over them, bring hither, and slay them before me." (Luke 19:27) Scholars agree that the Luke passage is to be taken literally, not as part of any parable.

So now, in addition to Jesus' own rather militant words, there is also the problem of Jesus' collaboration in all of the Old Testament murders. As part of the Triune God, Jesus was there at the dawn of creation, he was there during the Flood, and he was there during the Holocaust, while millions of prayers went unanswered. He is supposedly "there" right now, as terrorists blow each other up in holy wars, and Christians murder doctors who perform abortions. He supposedly will be "there" forever.

Most Christians believe that Jesus will be making a second

appearance on Earth, the much-awaited Second Coming. If he does, it would seem that the Gentle Carpenter from Galilee has a lot of explaining to do.

The "Christ-Killers"?

Anyone who has read a lot of books about the history of the Roman Catholic Church will necessarily have read a lot of books about anti-Semitism. The Catholic Church's centuries-long persecution of the Jews has always been accompanied by cries of the epithet, "Christ-killers!" Those words are still spit out, even today, by hateful bigots. The Jews, accused of killing Jesus, and therefore killing God, were guilty of the most horrible crime imaginable, deicide. Just think. They killed God.

This charge demands some scrutiny. The first thought that should spring to mind is, "How can you kill a *god?*" Isn't that by definition an impossibility? But setting aside this major assault on logic, anyone even slightly familiar with ancient Hebrew law knows that if the Jews had wanted to kill Jesus, for whatever reason, they would have stoned him to death. The Jews did not crucify people. The Romans did. That undeniable fact was skirted by claiming that the Jews *arranged* for Jesus' death and were therefore responsible for it, but they turned him over to the Roman authorities to do the actual killing. But how likely is that?

According to the gospels, Jesus was first brought to trial before the Sanhedrim, a sort of Jewish council of law, to be tried for blasphemy, a non-capital offense. This trial was supposedly held during the feast of the Passover, an impossibility, since no

Jewish trials were ever held during the Passover. Then, again according to the gospels, Jesus was passed here and there, enduring four trials in one day, finally ending up again, for the second time that day, in front of Pontius Pilate, the Roman procurator of Judea. The charge? Undoubtedly sedition, although the gospels are very unclear about this. The result? Pilate found Jesus to be totally free of any guilt. Then he promptly sentenced him to death. "Pilate saith unto them, Take ye him, and crucify him: for I find no fault in him." (John 19:6) Does this make any sense at all? Has any theologian ever thought this one through? Roman courts were known for their fairness. It is incomprehensible.

Even if the Jews were screaming for Jesus' blood, why would Pilate automatically do their bidding? Who ruled Judea, Pilate or the Jews? History leaves no doubt about that, so what was Pilate's motivation? Well, they say that Pilate was afraid that this trouble-maker, Jesus, might somehow start an insurrection, so he'd best be got rid of. But if that's true, then we're going to have to rewrite history.

The following is only a partial list of some of the Jewish and pagan writers who wrote at the time of Jesus or in the first century and a half of the Common Era. They made no mention of Jesus' supposedly astounding appearance on Earth. They include: Arrian, Epictetus, Favorinus, Josephus, Juvenal, Lucian, Martial, Persius, Petronius, Philo-Judaeus, Pliny the Elder, Pliny the Younger, Plutarch, Pompon Mela, Ptolemy, Quintilian, Seneca, Seutonius, Tacitus, and Valerius Maximus. The few doubtful mentions (such as that of Tacitus) are clearly references to what Christians believed, not that what they believed was *true.*

This list is far from comprehensive, but it still paints a vivid picture.

Why were there no contemporary writers to relate Jesus' miracles, his possible insurrection-leading, or the fact that when he died the sun stopped shining at midday, that there were earthquakes, and that graves opened up allowing corpses to emerge from them alive? You'd think someone would have noticed. These writers were writing about the place where Jesus supposedly lived, worked miracles, and then died so dramatically. But except for a few obvious Christian interpolations inserted clumsily a couple of centuries later, and universally acknowledged by scholars to *be* interpolations, these writers are silent about Jesus. How can this be?

Nevertheless, assuming that the Jews wanted Jesus dead and somehow forced a Roman procurator to kill him, and assuming further that no one writing at the time had heard anything about it, the most important question about this whole issue is this: why was Jesus supposedly sent to Earth in the first place? Every single Christian, including the little children, can answer that one. Jesus was sent to Earth to suffer and die for the sins of humankind. It was as a sacrificial lamb that he was sent.

Now think about this for a minute. Assume for the moment that the Jews were responsible for the suffering and death of Jesus. Shouldn't they be applauded? What do Christians want? Would they rather have it that Jesus had been allowed to live to a ripe old age, preaching about the Kingdom of God, eating his Passover meals, observing the Sabbaths, and then dying peacefully in his sleep from, say, a stroke? How would that have fulfilled Old Testament prophecies about a Messiah? Even if the

Jews had accepted Jesus as their true leader, like King David, what about his dying for the sins of humankind mission? How would he have carried that out?

Even if he had managed to carry out his mission by being killed by the Romans while being the truly recognized King of the Jews, wouldn't the only Jesus-worshipers today be Jews? After all, there are many stories in Jewish history about deposed kings, murdered kings, revolts and so on. But the rest of the world went blithely on its way, paying not the slightest attention to the upheavals *within* the Jewish community. So why would the death of this particular Jew (Jesus) have affected anyone other than Jews? Most probably, it would not have had any effect at all on non-Jews.

It seems Christians want it both ways. They want to believe that Jesus was sent to suffer and die for their sins, but they are furious that Jesus had to suffer and die for their sins. They bitterly resent his crucifixion. But why? *Someone* had to do it. Otherwise Christians would be in the bizarre position of having nothing to be Christian about. Jesus would have come and gone, like hundreds of other preacher-teachers of his time, not even a ripple in history, and we would all still be stuck here with no possible remission of our sins.

So the very idea of hurling "Christ-killer!" as an epithet is in itself a contradiction. It could almost be said that a proper greeting might be, "Did your ancestors crucify Christ for our sins? Bless them!"

There is never, in any age, any excuse for bigotry. But for Pope after Pope, century after century, to have engaged in the worst possible form of bigotry, persecution, is unconscionable.

St. John Chrysostom, in the fourth century, said, "I hate the Jews. God hates the Jews and always did." In 1555 Pope Paul IV published a Bull called *Cum nimis absurdum* that stressed that the "Christ-killers," the Jews, were by nature slaves and should be so treated. In 1581 Pope Gregory XIII claimed that the guilt of the Jews regarding the killing of Jesus grew deeper with successive generations, entailing perpetual slavery.

For four centuries the medieval Roman Catholic Inquisition rained terror on Europe. Whole communities of Jews were forced either to convert to Christianity or to leave the *country* the next day. Most "converted." Entire towns were baptized all at the same time. Then, if any of them were discovered observing any Jewish rites, they were hauled before the Catholic Inquisition for their "heresy," subjected to gruesome torture, and then burned at the stake. So if you liked to put on clean underwear every Saturday, or if you didn't like the taste of pork, you could be, and probably would be, tortured and then murdered by the Church.

The Catholic Church prefers not to look backward, and treats the Inquisition is as if it didn't happen. But it *did* happen, and thousands upon thousands of innocent people, a huge percentage of whom were Jews, were subjected to agonies we can barely imagine. It's difficult to find words to convey the ugliness of all this. That scores of professed religious leaders could condemn, with such venomous hatred, an entire ethnic group (along with all of their future offspring) for something that may or may not have happened centuries earlier, is almost unbelievable. The absurdity of it is exceeded only by its cruelty.

And it led straight to the gas chambers of Auschwitz.

Pope Pius XII kept his mouth tightly closed while those gas chambers at Auschwitz were working full time. The whole world knew what was going on, but the Pope spoke not one word against Hitler. His silence equated to aiding and abetting genocide. And as recently as 1965 Pope Paul VI preached a sermon in which he said that although the Jews were predestined to receive the Messiah, they not only failed to do so, but when Christ finally did arrive they slandered and then killed him. (If the Jews were predestined to receive Jesus as Messiah, how could they *not* have done so?) Paul VI seems to be just another in a very long line of anti-Semitic Popes. Will it never end?

The Catholic Church's history of strident anti-Semitism has been bloody and inexcusable. The victims of the Church's relentless, ruthless bigotry would fill a thousand cemeteries. And the terrible irony of it all is that the Jesus of their Bible — was a Jew.

7

Pandora's Box

The trouble with born-again Christians is that they are an even bigger pain the second time around.

Herb Caen, *San Francisco Chronicle*

Once you begin asking sound, logical questions about religion, you will soon find that, like unraveling a piece of thread from a delicate silk blouse, things begin to fall apart. Each new, forthright question leads to many other forthright questions, presenting you, literally, with a Pandora's box.

There are so many questions that cannot be answered logically about religion in general and Christianity in particular, that it is not surprising that many True Believers will not even tolerate their asking, let alone grapple for answers. But grapple they must. Just as extraordinary claims demand extraordinary proof, so extraordinary religious puzzles demand extraordinary explanations.

• If a plane crashes and ninety-nine people die while one survives, it is called a miracle. Should the families of the ninety-nine think so?

• If there's an earthquake and a house collapses and a man inside emerges unscathed it is called a miracle, since it's so unlikely. But if a woman is standing next to a church during a mild earthquake and just one brick from the steeple dislodges, falls and strikes her on the head, killing her instantly, why is this not also a miracle? It is just as unlikely. Her exact position, the exact position of the brick, the wind velocity and direction at the time and the precise moment of the quake all had to be exactly as they were or it wouldn't have happened at all. Isn't this a miracle?

• Do mentally retarded people go to Heaven?

• How can an all-merciful, loving god watch over the *eternal* agonies of his own creations in Hell?

• Supposedly the Jews were God's "Chosen People." How could God have favorites? How could God choose anyone over anyone else? And how were they chosen? Did they draw straws? How many groups were in the running? Such a human failing, having a favorite child, does not rest comfortably on a supposedly transcendent god.

• Why is God male? Why would an eternal, non-human, non-animal, non-reproducing, one-hundred-percent spiritual being require sexual gender?

• Jesus Christ is said to have been born to the Virgin Mary, who was made pregnant by God. Jesus was also supposedly descended from King David and Abraham, and the first verse of the first chapter of the first book of the New Testament sets about proving this. From "Abraham begat Isaac" right down to Jesus, every generation is accounted for. There is only one problem. The lineage is traced forward from Abraham to . . . Joseph! Joseph, Mary's husband, Jesus' stepfather, was said to have had no biological relationship with Jesus at all, Mary having been impregnated by the Holy Ghost. So how could Jesus possibly be related to Joseph's ancestors? Much is made of Jesus' supposed descent from David, since this kinship fulfills Old Testament prophecies, so such a glaring error is difficult to understand. If lineage can be traced through *stepparents*, then the word "lineage" has no meaning. The only plausible explanation here is that since women were considered too unimportant to confer kinship, the Holy Lineage simply had to be traced to a male, Joseph. Never mind that he was no more related to Jesus than your own Aunt Fannie. Such contempt for women stops just short of eliminating altogether the female role in reproduction, as happened in the Greek myth that has Athena being born straight from the head of Zeus. But the concept of Zeus giving birth from his own head is no more outrageous than the assertion that Jesus is descended from King David through his stepfather.

Save Yourselves!

Most religions involve the propitiation of one or more gods. Early humans took nature's twists and turns very personally, believing them to be the expressions of displeasure from their gods, rather than the natural phenomena that they really were. One way to get a volcano to stop erupting, some people thought, was to throw a live human being into it, thereby, hopefully, satisfying the blood-lust of the god believed to be living there. This grisly type of human sacrifice has a tragically long history, spanning the globe and spanning the ages. This connecting of human misfortune with godly anger has held universal appeal, and most religions are based on it.

Some of the Greek gods, like Zeus and Aphrodite, possessed some very human failings, so that this kind of anger/punishment/propitiation relationship between humans and god made some sense. It does not make sense, however, if you posit a loving, merciful, just and perfect god. Such a god could not possibly require sacrifices or take vengeance on his own creations.

Just as with the paradoxes involved in creation, the concept of "salvation" is fraught with difficulties. To begin with, just what are you supposed to be saved from? Hell, they say. Where did Hell come from? God created it for bad people. Where do bad people come from? God created them, too. Why? At this point the answers become convoluted.

True Believers will try to salvage their salvation theory by saying that God didn't create the bad things here — people did. They insist that people sin of their own free will, and if they'd straighten up and fly right, they wouldn't end up in Hell. But this argument fails for several reasons.

First of all, humans were supposedly created by God, "free will" and all. So if these free-willed people sin it is because God created them that way. And knowing all things, past, present and future (omniscience) he knew on the day he created humans that Hitler's Germany, for example, was going to be one of the results of those human creations. So if God didn't want Hitler's Germany to happen, he shouldn't have created the creatures whom he knew well in advance would bring it about.

Second, since God supposedly knows all there is to know, he will know, even before a person is born, whether or not that person will ultimately end up in Hell. And no matter how you play around with words, you will not change the fact that this equates to predestination. So whether or not anyone can be considered to be acting of his own free will is highly questionable. You can argue that God isn't *causing* your actions, but merely knows in advance what they'll be, so you are still able to choose freely. But the fact remains that before you drew your first breath of life, God supposedly knew with infallible certainty if you were bound for Hell. There will be nothing free in your actions. Omniscience means predestination, and predestination means that God arbitrarily saves some people and damns some people, reducing human beings to automatons and making God an ogre.

But even if the decision to damn were not arbitrary, the idea of a loving god creating a special place of eternal torment is repugnant. To imagine this god casting millions of his supposedly beloved "children" into this place of torment, forever, is inconceivable. So much for forgiveness. Talk about holding a grudge. The concept of Hell is barbaric and sadistic, and clearly betrays its primitive origins in the worship of fire-and-brimstone-belching volcanoes.

The Devil You Say

A little girl came home from school one day and announced to her Christian parents that she wanted to become Jewish. When asked to explain her surprising request, she answered that she had just learned that most Jews didn't believe in Hell, and this sounded like a much better deal all the way around. Indeed.

Satan. Lucifer. Beelzebub. The Evil One. The Prince Of Darkness. *The Devil.* These terms conjure up images of that other infamous character, "the Boogeyman," who has struck terror into the hearts of countless little children. I submit that the Devil and the Boogeyman are one and the same.

The idea of an evil, supernatural being doing terrible things to us mortals is an ancient and primitive one. It was used by our remote ancestors to explain what to them was otherwise inexplicable — sudden deaths, mysterious ailments and disappearances. Little children can certainly be understood for believing in such a monstrous-like creature if their parents are foolish and cruel enough to threaten them with it. But why do intelligent adults accept the concept of a Devil?

Why have we, generation after generation, scared the wits out of our children, as well as ourselves, with the belief in a Devil who will supervise our agony for all of eternity? Why do we do this to ourselves? While such irrational threats may serve as a partial deterrent to some people who have a penchant, say, for stealing, this crime-deterrent explanation falls short when you consider the absolutely horrific nature of the punishment. And history has shown that all of the "Devil's Gonna Get You" speeches have not had even the slightest effect on mass murderers or serial killers. So what's going on here?

If a child wants something that another child has, he will usually make a grab for it. The result will be either (a) he gets it and gloats, or (b) he doesn't get it and pouts. If the child makes a grab, loses, and then must also watch the coveted item go to a third party, a hated rival, there will be more than pouting. This may come to serious blows. Especially when it involves prized food items, children are cutthroats. If there is only one child involved, it will just be a matter of his whining and imploring until he either gets what he wants or you get him to shut up, whichever occurs first. But if there's more than one child involved, stand by.

Let's say there is a luscious piece of cake to be divided between two children. And let's say you are wise enough to employ the tactic of allowing one child to do the cutting while allowing the other to have first pick. You are going to see a protractor used here. If there are several children accepting cookie treats, and one thinks the cookies were counted out incorrectly, you will see human rivalry at its most intense.

So if little Johnny tries to grab from little Billy what he feels is his deserved Oreo, and in the fracas little Susie grabs it away from both of them and then wolfs it down, you will have an outraged Johnny. If Johnny hates Susie to begin with, because they're the same age but she can already beat him up, Johnny may have his first fleeting thoughts of homicide.

Now, if you take the howling Johnny off to one side and inform him that he should not be so upset because, at some unspecified place in some vague future, Susie will *get what's coming to her* (suffering) and, at that same time, Johnny will be rewarded with a ka-billion Oreos because he is so deserving, you are on your way to mollifying one ticked-off toddler. You've appealed to his innate sense of fairness and high self-esteem. It's all a pack of lies, of course, but the outraged tears may slacken a bit.

However, the dark side of this pack of lies is that if you insist that Susie will "get hers," you will have to follow through with this sick logic and inform Johnny that, yes, it's possible, if he's not careful, that he will also "get his."

Frightening children for the sole purpose of frightening them, as opposed to frightening them with ghost stories that entertain them, is a terrible thing to do. It should be viewed as a form of abuse. It's tragically simple to convince children of the existence of the Devil, just as it's easy to convince them of the existence of Santa Claus. This is no real challenge, Folks. As one theologian put it, give me a child until he's seven and he's mine for life.

But this is so very wrong. The fact that the Hitler Youth Movement succeeded so well should be evidence enough that any sort of dogmatic indoctrination of children before they reach the age of reason, is simply immoral. To lie to children about some pie-in-the-sky paradise for good little tots, can only give young minds a warped view of their fellow human beings, and will definitely encourage bigotry. To threaten them with the Devil if they're bad little tots is unconscionable. Let them keep that precious openness of mind that all children start out with, and let them decide about religion only after they are rational adults.

Of course, such a practice might mean the end of all religion as we know it. However, if that should prove true, it would mean that the religions were unworthy in the first place. Food for thought.

Growing up is hard enough without adults screaming about devils. Justice seems rare. Good people are seldom rewarded for their suffering, the meek will never inherit the earth, and wicked people often live in the lap of luxury, sometimes even at 1600 Pennsylvania Avenue. Life is not fair. That is not to say that we shouldn't try to make it as fair as possible, and all compassionate human groups do just that. But try as we might, we cannot eliminate all of the inequities.

This, most probably, is at the heart of the Devil concept. It isn't just a matter of wanting to negate the seeming pointlessness of our lives and deaths by postulating an eternal reward. In contrast to some religions that profess a well-led life to be its own reward, the Fire-and-Brimstone preachers, which represent a huge section of Christianity, spend *most* of their time railing about the Devil. And you can hear the ugly truth in their voices and see it in their eyes. It's not that they're so happy about going to Heaven. It's that they're so happy about the *rest of us* going to Hell. They're finally going to get even for all of life's unfairness.

No other explanation accounts for the incessant, wild-eyed haranguing about the Devil that is so common. If God is so loving, why don't Christians stick with that theme instead of graphically cataloging all of the Devil's horrible powers? How about, "God is love" and leave it at that? The centuries of Devil-talk have certainly not eliminated crime nor made our streets safe. However, if True Believers can ponder the eternal sufferings of all of their enemies, real or imagined, some of the sting is taken out of life's injustices. The Devil becomes their equalizer.

"Just you wait, you godless, life-enjoying, happy atheists (especially those of you who have more money than *I* do). You're gonna get yours!" This may be an ugly and ignoble concept, but many human emotions are ugly and ignoble.

So fundamentalists continue to try literally to scare the hell out of their own children, and attempt the same with the rest of us. Their frightened children deserve our sympathy, but it is hard to imagine losing any sleep over a horned, pitchforked piece of sadistic extortion. In fact, we would all do well to take the eminently sound logic of the little-girl-who-would-be-Jewish one step further. Let's choose the universe with no Devil, Hell *or* God in it.

Now I Lay Me Down To Sleep

School prayer. What a lot of information is packed into those two little words! It can polarize like few other issues. If you doubt it, throw that phrase out at your next cocktail party and then stand back and watch the fur fly.

School prayer. The futility of prayer itself is dealt with elsewhere and is not the issue here. The issue is why is there such a push to introduce prayer into public schools? Who stands to gain or lose with public school prayer?

First of all, it must be pointed out, loudly and clearly, that you can pray anywhere and any time you please without involving anyone else. Well, almost any time. It *is* difficult to get in any quality praying while you're sleeping, or under general anesthetic, or flossing your teeth. But generally speaking prayer is an easily accomplished act. No props required. You have your own built-in, do-it-yourself kit.

So how can fundamentalists make the outlandish assertion that Christian students are being prevented from praying in school because there is no official "moment of prayer"? That's like saying that students are being prevented from scratching an itch because there is no official "moment of scratching." Go ahead, scratch. Go ahead, pray.

Christians aren't fighting for their children to be allowed to pray in school. They already have that unfettered ability. No, what they want is to force *your* children to acknowledge *their* god. It's a power play all the way. That supposedly innocuous "moment of silence" is a deafening roar to a nonbeliever. There is no doubt in anyone's mind what that moment is for. It is intended to honor the Christian god at the beginning of the school day, as prayer is often used this way at the start of any endeavor. And this cannot be tolerated.

Fundamentalists make lame, condescending and totally unconvincing arguments about how Jews, Muslims and others are free to pray to their own gods or not pray at all. Bull. When your child is forced to participate in a moment of silence while her classmates close their eyes and silently move their lips in praise of their god, she is being coerced into participating in the acknowledgment of a deity. And no amount of sophistry in semantics can change this simple fact. James Madison would have pitched a fit.

But why are they pushing so hard for this? The federal

deficit, starving babies, civil wars and terrorists seem the more proper considerations for our Congress. And of course it could be argued that nonbelievers are themselves making too big a fuss over one lousy minute of school prayer. However, what we have here is called a "foot in the door." Anyone who truly believes that all fundamentalists really want is this one "moment of silence," needs a reality check.

My father was a highly intelligent, well-read man, with far-reaching interests and a wonderfully dry sense of humor. He was a kind man. And he ardently supported school prayer. He backed Christianity's "The Lord's Prayer" as the best candidate for use in all public schools. Incredulously, I asked him about the rights of non-Christians, since we both knew my best friend was Buddhist. He dismissed that obstacle with a flick of the wrist and the comment that there weren't enough non-Christians to worry about. I was mystified.

I teasingly offered my own candidate for school prayer. I suggested, "Now I lay me down to sleep. I pray the Lord my soul to keep. If I should die before I wake, I pray the Lord my soul to take. Amen." My father didn't laugh. I then asked if he would approve of students being asked to recite the Roman Catholic prayer, "Hail, Mary, full of grace, blessed art thou among women. . . ." His Missouri Synod Lutheran eyes flashed anger at me and conveyed utter disbelief that any offspring of his could even suggest anything so offensive and so *dumb*. (To this day I do not see any difference in offering either of those prayers for public school use.) We agreed to disagree.

It is often a struggle to reconcile high intelligence with powerful religious beliefs. But it must be done. No one is accusing

Newt Gingrich, who proposed a Constitutional Amendment allowing school prayer, of being stupid. But how can it be that some of us embrace, enthusiastically, all kinds of religious stories and rules, some making no sense at all, while others of us ask insightful questions and begin the doubting process? Why do we differ so?

Perhaps it has something to do with our ages, with the number of years we are "protected" from unbelieving influences. My own religious questions, and therefore doubts, began as soon as my friendship with my Buddhist girlfriend developed, when I was around twelve or thirteen years old. Language teachers will tell you that teaching young children to speak two or three different languages is fairly easy, while teaching adults is much more difficult. Many immigrants learn English from their children. A young brain is a malleable brain. And, perhaps, an older brain is just no longer open to new ideas, especially if these ideas challenge some very comforting pie-in-the-sky beliefs, and if the early indoctrination was powerful to begin with. Indoctrinate a child early enough and *strongly* enough, with little or no outside distraction, and maybe you will end up with an ardent adult Believer, unlikely ever to change.

If this is correct, school prayer is suddenly brought back into sharp focus. Without school prayer, a young child might ask a logical but dangerous question such as, "Daddy, how come we don't say a prayer before lunch at school?" Well, Dad, how come? School prayer *reinforces* religious beliefs for Christians as well as coercing nonbelievers. "Stay, don't stray" is the constant entreaty of fundamentalists as they try to protect their children from any possible "contamination" by freethought. In our nonhomogenous society, such "contamination" (like my Buddhist friend) presents a very real threat for Christians. Thus school prayer becomes a tool for fundamentalists in convincing their children that their fundamentalist principles are correct. ("You pray at school, don't you? Well, that just proves our point.") School prayer will help discourage awkward questions, and curiosity is the natural enemy of religious belief.

But the bottom line here is that if Christians are insecure about their hold over their own children, that is just too damn bad. Public schools were never intended to be a teaching tool for Christianity or any other religion, nor should they be. History has recorded the atrocious failures of all theocracies. We live in a democracy founded upon the wise doctrine of separation of church and state. It must remain so.

Amen.

The Question Of Evil

There are two kinds of evil in this world, and they both cause human suffering. The most widely recognized is "moral" evil, which results from human actions — murder, rape, war and so on. The other is "natural" evil which results from disasters, like earthquakes or plagues, and leaves people dead or disabled. The fact that evil exists at all, let alone so abundantly, presents a thorny problem for Christians and their god. And so far, they haven't been able to resolve it.

If God created the entire universe, and evil is part of that universe, then God must have created evil. For centuries this conundrum has been posed:

(1) If God did not know there would be evil in his universe, he could not be omniscient (all-knowing).

(2) If God knew there would be evil but could do nothing to prevent it, he could not be omnipotent (all-powerful).

(3) If God knew there would be evil but chose to do nothing to prevent it, he could not be omnibenevolent (all-good).

The argument that humankind's volitional actions, which spring from our "free will," are the cause of evil and therefore not God's fault, fails as soon as you ask where that free will came from. It came from God. And it changes the trio of propositions only slightly. "If God did not know that creating humans with a free will would result in evil. . . ."

And it must be emphasized again that if God wanted people who would not do evil, he should have created people who would not do evil. Nothing could have prevented an all-powerful god from creating perfect, evil-free people if that's what he had wanted. To argue that without free will we would then be zombies or automatons, is to assume facts not in evidence. We have no idea what we'd be like without free will. And in any case, whether God had wanted evil-free zombies or evil-free non-zombies, there would have been nothing to prevent him, in his omnipotence, from creating either kind of creature.

The argument that God will punish all evildoers in some afterlife, therefore making everything turn out all right in the end, is to ignore the very real suffering of the innocent victims of those evildoers. If you beat your dog until he's bloody and whimpering, and then give him a nice, big ham bone later as an apology, or if you punish yourself, it will not remove the animal's pain or change the evil nature of what you've done. The proposition of eternal punishment for wicked people does not eliminate the terrible suffering of their innocent victims in the first place.

One desperate, though creative, attempt to explain away evil argues that humans can't tell the difference between good and evil, since we're merely mortal. Perhaps, they say, what we perceive as evil is not really evil. But if that's true, then Christians cannot claim that their god is all-good, since Christians, as mere mortals, can't recognize good or evil.

Blaming Satan for all evil also fails, for two reasons. First, the trio of propositions once again changes only slightly. "If God didn't know that Satan would be part of his created universe. . . ." Second, if you claim God cannot be held responsible for Satan's actions because he did not create him, Satan somehow being present before creation, then you are now faced with a two-deity universe, which thoroughly contradicts the concept of One True God, Creator of All Things.

The natural or physical evils must also be reconciled with an all-merciful god. It has been argued that such disasters, like an enormous earthquake, bring out the best in humans as we rush aid to the victims. But this argument callously overlooks the terrible sufferings of the unfortunate victims while the rest of us are learning our little lesson in caring. If this is God's way of teaching us to be compassionate, he is choosing a cruel, heartless way to do it.

Jack the Ripper, Stalin, Ivan the Terrible, the Hillside Strangler, Attila the Hun, Hitler, Son of Sam and so on, are all grisly proof that evil inhabits our world. Starving children, raped children and battered children are further corroboration. So are the

San Andreas Fault, Mt. Vesuvius, and the hurricane season. The lists could go on forever, but the point has been made. Just how can all of these horrors, these "evils," be consistent with an all-loving god who created all that there is?

If God did in fact create this world, if he is truly all-merciful, and if he does participate in human affairs, then the preceding lists should not be possible. They should not exist. That sort of evil could not exist in a world that is watched over by a loving god who has the power to stop it at any time, if he so chooses.

If humans can understand the concept of innocent victims and cruel suffering, then an all-knowing god must surely understand even *more*. If we are moved to pity when we see human suffering, then an all-merciful god must be moved even *more*. Humans, by definition, cannot see, feel or understand as much as God. (Of course, we can feel envy and greed, which God supposedly cannot feel, so doesn't that mean we are capable of something God is not capable of? Well, that's another story.) In beholding the incalculable sufferings of innocents in the world, surely God must feel so much pity as to be moved to end it all. If not, he's not as loving as we are. For, if any of a countless number of us had the power, we would certainly eliminate all evil and end the desperate suffering in this world.

This question of evil has never been answered satisfactorily, and, within the constraints of formal religions, it never will be. As long as the world is awash with evil, we know that there is no all-merciful, all-powerful, all-knowing god watching over us. It's as simple as that.

8

Doing Good

The last temptation is the greatest treason:
To do the right deed for the wrong reason.

T. S. Eliot, *Murder in the Cathedral*

Would morality disappear in the absence of a god? Before you can answer that question you must first define morality, which is not as easy as it sounds. If you consider the generally accepted definition as conforming to society's concept of what is right or proper behavior, you then are faced with the startling proposition that a member of the Aztec culture who enthusiastically cut out the hearts of live human victims was behaving morally. Their society, after all, considered human sacrifice a religious rite, obviously right and proper behavior. If you consider morality to be a matter of obeying "God's laws," we still have the problem with the Aztecs, or any other sacrificing society, who considered themselves to be serving their god, and therefore behaving morally.

Different cultures in different eras produced widely divergent rules, some of which would seem barbaric or ridiculous to us today, but were nevertheless considered perfectly fair in their time. Our own American heritage includes the Rule of Thumb carried over from English common law, which dictated that a man could not beat his wife with any rod or stick that was thicker than his own thumb. This rule was considered to be the very embodiment of enlightenment and the batterer who flogged his wife by the hour was nevertheless considered properly moral as long as he used the right-sized stick. Apparently congratulations were in order if no bones were broken. Then, too, generations of God-fearing people who owned slaves considered themselves perfectly moral. It *was* legal, remember?

Defining morality, then, can be a difficult business, dependent totally on who is doing the defining. However, since our own Founding Fathers did such a shabby job of it by failing to condemn slavery or wife-beating, there is no reason to feel intimidated in trying a brand-new definition. Perhaps morality should simply be defined as behaving in such a way as to intentionally avoid hurting other people. Immorality would then be any course of action that intentionally hurts other people.

Quibblers will immediately ask whether or not, by this definition, spanking a child would be immoral. Or incarcerating a murderer. Or performing an emergency amputation without the benefit of anesthetics. But common sense can easily overcome these obstacles with cost/benefit ratios taken into account. And in any case this definition of morality declares that human sacrifice, wife-beating, slavery (and torture, such as that engaged in by the Roman Catholic Inquisition) are wrong, which is more than past definitions have done.

This definition also includes as moral such things as masturbation, consensual adult homosexuality, prostitution, gambling and drinking. As long as these activities do not hurt anyone else, they are moral. They might hurt you, of course, but as long as you hurt no one else — fine. Just as overeating can only hurt the person doing it, and therefore cannot be considered a matter of morality, so it should be with all other activities. Also, with this new definition, telling lies falls beautifully into either category, moral or immoral, depending on intent. (I love your new hat, Grandma!)

But whatever your definition of morality, the question of whether or not it would exist at all is always posed every time the question of God comes up. If there is no god, the question demands, then why not kill yourself? Why not kill someone else? Why not steal? Torture? And so on.

The fact that suicide, murder, theft and torture are all very well represented today among supposedly God-fearing people, and were even enthusiastically promoted by Christian clergy (shall we remember the Crusades? the Inquisition?) is somewhat beside the point here. The question here is, if there is *no* god, why *shouldn't* you commit murder? No one is asking why murder happens anyway, even though there supposedly is a god, although that's a very good question. But supposedly murder and theft would be engaged in by everyone, constantly, unless there were the staying hand of a god who threatens us with a Hell snapping at our heels if we don't refrain from such activities. But would we all be bloodthirsty killers without a god? Well, would we?

Human conduct obviously affects human communities. Why not kill your neighbor? Because any human group (or animal group, for that matter) that does not possess powerful taboos against the murdering of its own kind will simply not survive. Our remote ancestors had enough to deal with as it was. Harsh climate, disease, starvation and predation by other animals killed them off with chilling efficiency in any event, and if they had been busy knocking each other off at the same time, they wouldn't have survived long enough even to develop the concept of a god. Likewise, stealing, even though it is a far less serious problem, will cause feuds and in-fighting and will discourage all incentive if it is not controlled. Stealing is a taboo because it causes chaos, not because it will result in some dire punishment, handed out by an irate god, after we are dead and gone.

Just as it is impossible to pass on the trait of sterility to your children, it is very difficult to pass on the disposition toward suicide. If it takes very little to push you to that brink of self-destruction, you will more than likely not raise many offspring who could pass that trait on to their own children. Suicide occurs so seldom not because we are afraid of a vengeful god, but because we are descended from only those hardy ancestors whose instinct for self-preservation was so healthy and intact that even life's cruelest challenges could not dim their desire to carry on. The truly faint of heart were quickly removed from the gene pool ages ago and are ancestral to none of us.

Why does a mother lion handle her cubs so gently, so tenderly? Why does she let them chew on her tail? Why does she share her kills with them? It is not because it makes life easier or more pleasant for *her*. And it's not because she wants her species to survive. It is simply because her own mother did these things and she inherited those instincts from her, as her mother did from *her* mother. There may have been all sorts of lionesses who didn't give a rap about child care. Of course all their babies would have died and been unavailable to pass that carelessness on to *their* offspring.

Mother Nature has always been a demanding teacher. For most of the history of life on Earth, if a creature did something really stupid, it died. We humans have learned to mitigate, somewhat, some of life's pitfalls. We don't necessarily die anymore from a compound fracture of a leg, for example, and we've taught ourselves how to safely amputate limbs and so on. However, if you fall off the edge of a canyon rim you will more than likely die just as you would have a million years ago. Mother Nature is still at the ready with her deadly serious reminders to pay attention.

But inclinations or dispositions toward certain behavior can only take you so far. Do most people have to struggle with a frequent, powerful impulse to do murder? No. Do some people have this problem? Yes. And they must be dealt with.

Then there is the problem of raising children, who will do almost anything they think is in their own interest, only giving thought to those actions much later, probably while being yelled at by an adult. They also need rules. As human groups developed culture, rules evolved. They would have to or chaos would reign and Mother Nature, that tough old bitch, is always willing to hurl into oblivion any group stupid enough to turn all its aggressions on itself. Cooperation between humans, as with many other animals, is almost a prerequisite for survival, and all human groups have had some sort of rules.

The concept of "god" apparently came into this arrangement very early on, since every human culture yet discovered found that gods of some sort were required to explain life's mysteries. The sun, the moon, the planets, volcanoes, rivers, trees, rock formations, jaguars, falcons, cows, bulls, snakes, jackals, panthers, eagles, crocodiles, crabs, the spirit in the lake, the spirit in the sky, the spirit in the forest, the spirit in the cave, the goddess of fertility, the god of thunder, the god of lightning and our own ancestors, have all been worshipped at some time or other. We seem to have a deep-seated need to look up to someone. But morality (which is just a word for getting along with our fellow humans) was on the scene long before gods entered the picture. Had it not been, extinction would have embraced our intelligent, greedy, lusty, egoistic species before humankind's first prayer had ever been uttered. Once gods had been created it was only natural to incorporate society's rules into the worship of those gods, giving the rules a bit of extra authority above and beyond just saying, "Don't do it because we say so!" Invoking higher authority in order to alter behavior is a common and generally successful practice, although the higher authority doesn't necessarily have to be real. Parents use Santa Claus in this way all the time.

Behaving Yourself

The Bible goes on and on, verse after chapter after page, in tedious detail, about what foods can and cannot be eaten and how those foods should be prepared, all accompanied by dire warnings. Why?

For example, in the Old Testament book of Leviticus is a forty-seven verse harangue about what foods are or are not an "abomination." It reads, in part:

"And the LORD spake unto Moses and to Aaron, saying unto them, Speak unto the children of Israel, saying, These are the beasts which ye shall eat among all the beasts that are on the earth. Whatsoever parteth the hoof, and is clovenfooted, and cheweth the cud, among the beasts, that shall ye eat. Nevertheless these shall ye not eat of them that chew the cud, or of them that divide the hoof: as the camel, because he cheweth the cud, but divideth not the hoof; he is unclean unto you." (Leviticus 11:1–4)

"And the hare, because he cheweth the cud, but divideth not the hoof; he is unclean unto you. And the swine, though he divide the hoof, and be clovenfooted, yet he cheweth not the cud; he is unclean to you." (11:6,7)

"And these are they which ye shall have in abomination among the fowls; they shall not be eaten, they are an abomination: the eagle, and the ossifrage, and the osprey, And the vulture, and the kite after his kind;" (11:13,14)

"And the stork, the heron after her kind, and the lapwing, and the bat." (11:19)

❖ ❖ ❖

"These also shall be unclean unto you among the creeping things that creep upon the earth; the weasel, and the mouse, and the tortoise after his kind, And the ferret, and the chameleon, and the lizard, and the snail, and the mole." (11:29,30)

❖ ❖ ❖

And so on. For over one thousand one hundred words, these warnings continue. Immediately preceding this section is a description of *where* certain food should be eaten. The proper place for eating a "sin offering" is specified.

❖ ❖ ❖

"And Moses spake unto Aaron, and unto Eleazar and unto Ithamar, his sons that were left, Take the meat offering that remaineth of the offerings of the LORD made by fire, and eat it without leaven beside the altar: for it is most holy: And ye shall eat it in the holy place, because it is thy due, and thy sons' due, of the sacrifices of the LORD made by fire: for so I am commanded" (Leviticus 10:12,13)

❖ ❖ ❖

"And Moses diligently sought the goat of the sin offering, and, behold, it was burnt: and he was angry with Eleazar and Ithamar, the sons of Aaron which were left alive, saying, Wherefore have ye not eaten the sin offering in the holy place, seeing it is most holy, and God hath given it you to bear the iniquity of the congregation, to make atonement for them before the LORD? Behold, the blood of it was not brought in within the holy place: ye should indeed have eaten it in the holy place, as I commanded." (Leviticus 10:16–18)

How many college students go home and burn a goat as a sin offering after cheating on midterms? Who really believes that a dead, burned animal can "bear the iniquity of the congregation?" Such primitive sacrifices and dietary laws are an embarrassment to anyone who claims that the Bible is the perfect moral guide, intended for all of humankind in any era. The lesson to be learned from the story of the *Three Little Pigs* is far more relevant to the human experience than any of these bewildering dietary rules.

To place dietary laws in the category of morality is insane. In the moral scope of things, who on earth cares if someone eats bacon along with eggs? Why should anyone care? Why should you be considered immoral if you eat a tortoise, or moral if you refrain from eating a bat? Such laws deserve only baffled disdain, and certainly should not be classified with laws of morality.

For a long, long time, the only accepted explanation for moral behavior was the fear of being brutalized by vengeful gods. But there is a lot more involved in moral behavior than just fear of divine retribution. Safe, secure, cooperating human groups are going to thrive, while wantonly savage groups will doom themselves. This guiding principle has been at work for all of history, just as it is today. There can be no denying the senseless slaughters that have dotted human history from the beginning, but this is not to say that most of us behave, or even want to behave, so savagely. The unbridled aggression that people always cite as proof of our intrinsic savagery is always a result of the few leading the many, and often those following have no desire to be where they are.

For example, most of the soldiers who have served in most of the wars would much rather have been anywhere else than where they were, being forced to kill other people. They would much rather have been at home with their wives and children, enjoying life as best they could. To be sure, there have always been violent men, and there probably always will be, but they do not represent the rest of us. This principle can be tested fairly easily.

Consider your fellow humans. You have been living among thousands of these large omnivorous "killers" all of your life. Now. When was the last time you saw someone murder someone else? Or even attack someone else? When was the last time you, personally, really felt like killing someone? We all use hyperbole: "I'll kill him when he gets home!" But when was the last time you honestly had to struggle with the very powerful impulse to go up to someone and extinguish his life? As sickening as our crime rate is, these murderous impulses do not occur in *most* of us *most* of the time. They are rare. And it is not the intellectual conviction that a vengeful god will do horrible things to us in some afterlife that prevents us from killing each other at the drop of a hat. It is just that most of us never seriously even consider the act of murder. It does not appeal.

The prevalence of the impulse to commit certain acts will be in direct inverse proportion to the amount of harm such acts would do to a human community. That is, the more harmful a behavior is, the less likely it is you'll want to do it in the first place. Mother Nature, in her winnowing-out process referred to elsewhere, will not tolerate wanton murder as the rule rather than the exception. After you've all killed each other off, she'll clear the stage for some other group to try its hand at survival, and if they prize their lives highly, they will probably succeed. So even though terrible people do terrible things to other people, as we all know too well, the vast majority of us do not, nor do we want to.

Murder, then, which is a devastating act not only for the victim but for society as a whole, is also not very appealing. We'd rather not do it. If you look at all of society's rules this way a definite pattern will emerge. The more harmful an action would be to society, the less likely it is you would want to do it anyway.

Suicide is also a defeating act for all concerned and, once again, is not very appealing. Aside from the occasional, dramatic, depressed fantasy wherein we lament, "They'll be sorry when I'm dead and gone!" how many of us really, seriously plan our own death? Very, very few of us. Declaring suicide to be against the law, however, is inane and is based solely on the religious view that holds suicide to be a sin.

Stealing, which is nowhere near as harmful to society as is murder, is proportionately more appealing. It is far more common, and many more of us do in fact have to struggle with the temptation to acquire that which is not ours to acquire.

Kidnapping, much more serious again, is also much less appealing. Pushing, shoving, slapping and fighting in general cause little harm to society within certain limits, so it is, to the dismay of many of us, an often appealing outlet for anger.

Rape, which is an act of violence using sex as a weapon, is

very harmful to the victim. Many people confuse the act of rape with the act of sex. They are not the same thing. Men do not rape because they want sex. They rape because they want to hurt a woman and they use sex to do it.

A woman's stark terror, powerlessness, humiliation and pain are what the rapist is after, not a jolly roll in the hay. He does not want to arouse. He wants to hurt. Men do not rape because they are horny. A sexually aroused man can always find a willing partner, even if he has to pay for it. But even if that plan falls through, the idea of grabbing a woman, flinging her to the ground and scaring the hell out her, hurting her while trying to stifle her terrified screams, does not appeal to a normal, healthy, aroused man. Masturbation will be far more appealing. No, men rape because they crave the violence inherent in the act and the powerful sense of control over a woman that rape produces. They want to hurt.

However, because so much misinformation about rape has been disseminated for so long (she was "asking" for it; if you can't avoid it, might as well enjoy it), rape and sex have become blurred in many minds. We continue to promote this confusion, mostly through TV, movies and novels, by depicting rape victims as beautiful, as if their attractiveness were somehow the cause of the rape. This false image of rape victims, which is completely misleading since stocky, older women are also victimized, serves further to confuse.

Rape is brutal and you must *be* brutal to carry it out. You must plan your rape so as to avoid witnesses. Then you must threaten, with or without a weapon, to hurt or even kill your victim if she fights you. *You must mean this.* You may have to hit her to force her into place. You are now faced with a completely terrified woman who is either screaming or crying or both, or who maybe is struggling to control her sobs of terror. She will probably beg you not to do this, pleading for you not to hurt her. In her fear she may vomit or lose bladder or bowel control. If there has been any scuffle at all she will be bleeding.

So there you are, looking down at this terrified creature with a tear-stained face, her pupils dilated with fear, begging you for mercy or mute with horror. She is in pain, she is awash with humiliation, paralyzed with fear, and pleading with you not to murder her. If you are a man and you can honestly say that this pathetic image is sexually arousing, then you have a serious problem and professional help is urgently required. But most men will not find this scenario arousing. Most men would feel the desire to scoop up this poor woman in their arms, wrap her in a warm blanket, and then beat the bejeesus out of the son of a bitch who did this to her.

The frequency with which murder accompanies rape is further evidence of its violent nature. The rapist/murderer is, sadly, a real feature of the real world, as the late and unlamented Ted Bundy demonstrated. So even though men often "joke" about rape, and even though the Bible gives it a wink and a nod, rape is an act of violence, not sex. The Bible may consider rape to be part of the "spoils" of war, but civilized societies consider it a serious crime.

And so, as you continue down the list of different types of offensive behavior, the pattern is fairly clear. The worse the crime is for society, the less likely most of us are to want to do the thing in the first place. Maladaptive behavior tends to breed itself out of populations, as it were, and we write laws to take care of those stubbornly maladaptive people who don't possess inhibitions toward such behavior. This admittedly simplified generalization breaks down completely when it comes to sexual behavior.

Most of our laws regarding sexual behavior are based on religious laws, some of which are incredible. Since homosexual activity produces no offspring, most of us are descended primarily from people with definite heterosexual orientations. The constant religious harping against it is really unnecessary, since it is not appealing to the vast majority of us anyway. So far, so good. There are still many states in this country that have laws against adultery. Those of us who like to think we have real separation of church and state would do well to look at these laws that carry *prison terms* for adultery. The separation is not as complete as we think. Then there is the admonition against engaging in sex with animals. This is a piece of cake for most of us, as very few of us feel sexual arousal when confronted with a Great Dane or a goat. Such bizarre activity is maladaptive, leading, fortunately, to no offspring, so most of us don't want to do it.

But now we enter the realm of pre-marital and extra-marital sex and we have ourselves a whole new ball game. Pre-marital and extra-marital sex in no way threaten the success of a population. Quite the contrary, the more sex the merrier, so to speak. Sex means babies and babies mean the success of a species and Mother Nature is in there pitching on this one. We do like our sex. We are attracted to, and want to be attractive to, lots of different people in a lifetime. Monogamy is an uphill climb all the way. Our record in this area is more or less disastrous and always has been. This is where the relationship between crimes and inclinations appears to break down. If you consider promiscuity a crime, as most religions do, you can't count on any innate reluctance to help you with this one. Just the opposite is true. As a form of entertainment sex is probably second to none, and many of us would argue that the only thing more important than sex is breathing.

However, there is really no contradiction here. Categorizing promiscuity as a crime is a totally arbitrary, totally religious, totally ridiculous thing to do. Prostitution is also a crime for religious reasons and none other. Sex between consenting adults, unless you are breaking a personal vow to a loved one, or creating a life you will not take responsibility for, hurts no one. So the relationship between our inclinations and those activities that hurt society, holds up after all. Promiscuity that hurts no one is a completely moral activity. Mother Nature wants to see as much of it as possible, and we find it very appealing indeed.

Screams of outrage are inevitable at this point. All these sexual goings-on, so the religious argument goes, will destroy The American Family, and ultimately society as a whole. But will they really? If that were true, the family would have ceased to exist ages ago. Like head colds and arthritis, promiscuity and prostitution have always been with us. We're just more honest about it now.

And in any event the notion of coercing people to behave morally is absurd. Threats of punishments, religious or secular, may indeed force someone to refrain from certain activities, and sometimes such coercion is necessary for the safety of citizens.

But make no mistake about it, those activities, or lack of them, are not moral choices. They represent coerced cooperation only. This seeming hairsplitting represents an important distinction. If one person refrains from robbing a bank only because he is afraid of getting caught, while another refrains because he truly believes it is wrong, then we have coerced cooperation in the first case and a moral decision in the second. The overall benefit to society is the same in either case, and if we behave decently toward each other the reasons why may be unimportant. But if a thoroughly abused child grows up to be a quiet, unassuming, cooperative citizen, wasn't the price tag too high? In a wholesome human community the reasons for approved behavior should matter to us.

Of course it is true that we coerce children constantly. We threaten and punish and struggle to turn our children into decent human beings, a feat that many beleaguered parents often believe to be impossible. And if a four-year-old starts to do something but then looks over her shoulder and changes her mind, we would not call this a moral choice. She just doesn't want to be yelled at again.

And yet, somewhere along the line, children, most of them, do begin to develop a sense of right and wrong. It may show itself in something like the teasing of a handicapped child. Your six-year-old may have seen others do it. She may know that there are no witnesses at the moment to get her in trouble if she decides to do it herself. She may even have laughed at the childishly cruel prank she witnessed earlier. But for some reason she doesn't do it. Her hand is not stayed because of some complicated theory about Heaven and Hell and sin and damnation.

She just doesn't think it would be *kind.* She has made a moral choice.

Arguments still rage hot and heavy about which is the most important influence in the life of a person — Nature or Nurture, Heredity or Environment, Genes or Jails — and the answer will undoubtedly turn out to be some complex combination. After all, we are not toy soldiers stamped out of a single mold. An abusive environment that causes one child to turn off and drop out, spurs another on to greatness. Just why some of us have such well-developed consciences while others of us are completely without them, is a mystery. Theories abound. Consciences are beaten into us, some believe, while others claim that, quite the contrary, consciences are beaten out of us. Still others appeal to genetics (the fruit never falls far from the tree) and of course there is the predictable standby about the devil making you do it. Someday we may know the answers, and genetics will undoubtedly play a large role in those answers, reaffirming the common sense notion that we are *not* ushered into this world as blank slates, waiting only to be molded by our environments. Any mother of more than one child can testify to their differing temperaments that manifest themselves almost from the delivery room. And no amount of environmental molding could have created Mozart or Einstein without some fancy footwork in the DNA department. However, once again in response to Mother Nature's prodding, most of us do have these often inconvenient consciences.

Consider robbing a bank. Morality implies choice and you may easily choose not to rob the bank, so choice is obvious. It is also a high risk kind of activity, capture and punishment being very possible. Will you refrain from doing it solely because of the possible consequences or because you just think it is wrong? A lot of us will struggle with this one, privately of course, as that fantasy of the perfect crime including $1,000,000 in untraceable cash and a one-way ticket to the South Pacific nudges its way into our consciousness. But this isn't really a fair test for morality. Robbing a bank doesn't really seem like robbing people. It is, of course, but it nevertheless doesn't *seem* like it. So let's consider a different scenario.

Let's consider robbing a family, a husband and wife with three children. Let's further imagine that you will be stealing all of this family's cash, cars, clothing, their actual house and all of their insurance policies so that when you're finished, they are destitute. (Obviously, you can't steal a house or insurance coverage, but for this argument assume that you can.) Now, with the same lure of South Pacific splendor, will you refrain from doing this solely because of the possible consequences or because you also think it just isn't *right?* You will probably feel a lot different about this robbery, and if you do, good for you. This is what morality is all about — our treatment of other people.

Same To You, Fella!

If you walk up to someone and slap him across the face, more than likely he will slap you right back. You learn this when you're about two. You don't like being slapped, so you think twice about doing it to someone else. The so-called Golden Rule ("Do unto others as you would have them do unto you"), which predates Christianity, is nothing more than the logical end product of this slap/slap-back observation. Every mother who has ever struggled with a quarrelsome toddler has asked, in exasperation, "Well, how would you like it if someone did that to *you*?" Humans have been asking this question of themselves, and each other, since the beginning of time. It is the basis for all moral codes, and it requires no mystical, supernatural origin. It is common sense.

In a gregarious, social species like Homo Sapiens, where individuals are constantly in close contact, getting along, which *is* morality, is a necessity, not a social nicety. At first we get along because we don't want to be slapped back, but as we mature and learn to care about other individuals, our kindnesses are prompted by affection and concern, not just fear. To insist that humans can only show these kindnesses to each other if they are coerced into it by a threatening god is an insult. We have an enormous capacity for love and respect, and we can help our children realize that potential even without postulating devils with horns or hells with agonies. We can, and should, achieve morality without threatening our children with a god who will slap back.

This brief examination of the relationship between the Judeo-Christian religion and morality would seem to confirm the position that morality need not have its roots in religion, and that religion is most definitely not always moral. Beating a child with a rod, as approved of in the Bible, and the cold-blooded massacres of hundreds of thousands of people, including dashing infants to pieces, cannot be considered moral by any civilized standard.

So then, in answer to our earlier question about whether

morality would disappear in the absence of a god, we can state with certainty that at least in some instances it could only improve.

9

Is Anybody Out There?

. . . perhaps we shall have to colonize the stars before it is finally borne in upon us that God is not out there.

R. J. Hollingdale, *Thomas Mann: A Critical Study*

We don't like the idea of being alone in the universe. It's lonely here. Gods in the heavens, demons from Hell, visitors from outer space, visits from long-dead relatives, and magic fairies living in the garden, have all been created by humans for the same reasons — to end our aloneness and to elevate our self-esteem. This is a big place, this universe of ours, and we seem to rattle around here all by ourselves. The ancients had no idea how huge this universe is (we are only now getting a glimmer of it ourselves), but even at that the world was too big for them.

Surely, they thought, *someone* else is out there. It can't just be us and a few lousy plants and animals. So, the ancients put gods in the skies and demons in Hell, and we have been happily engaged in this business ever since.

Having done so, we were not only no longer alone, but we were important. After all, if gods and devils, who have magical powers and everything, are willing to take the time to get involved in our lives, then we *must* be important. Even when the involvement seemed to be of the negative sort, like striking someone with a terrible ailment, humans could and did take some comfort in the belief that at least someone was paying attention to them and trying to convey some sort of message. Like a small child who can no longer tolerate being ignored, and intentionally kicks up a fuss though he knows he'll be punished, because even negative attention is better than no attention, so humankind has always demanded to be noticed. An indifferent universe is intolerable. Our egos will not permit it.

This aspect of human nature is nowhere more apparent than in our tenacious hold on our religions. Never mind that all of the world's religions are mutually exclusive. Never mind that millions of people have been murdered over these supposedly lofty religions. No, we still cling to our religious beliefs like toddlers to their teddy bears. And, since we humans are still in our infancy, as evidenced by our temper tantrums and our petulant, war-making approach to problem solving, the analogy is a good one. But someday, hopefully soon, we will grow up and realize that we can't look to the skies for the answers to our problems. The answers can only come from within us.

Some of the less sophisticated True Believers, who have no

My parents, LaVerne Kruggel and Edmund Meyer, at some unknown date. My mother still had her beautiful smile. Dad was attracted to her vivacious personality, and her big, jolly family. It was a stark contrast to his own somber life.

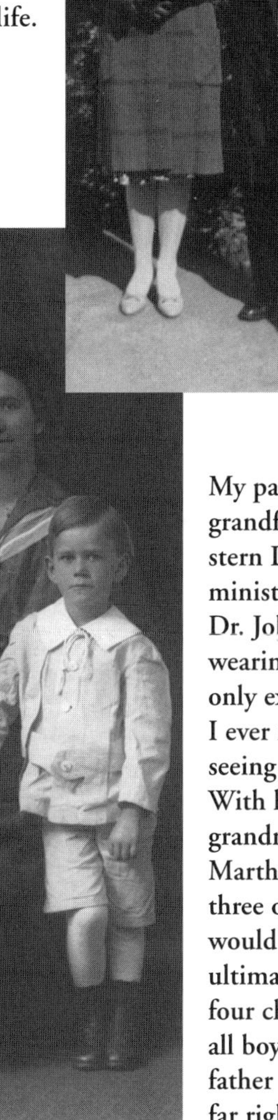

My paternal grandfather, the stern Lutheran minister, Dr. John Meyer, wearing the only expression I ever recall seeing on him. With him, my grandmother, Martha, and three of what would ultimately be four children, all boys. My father is on the far right.

The organ loft at Grand Lake Lutheran Church, where I literally spent half of my childhood. My father could play any pipe organ in existence. He was a wonderful musician.

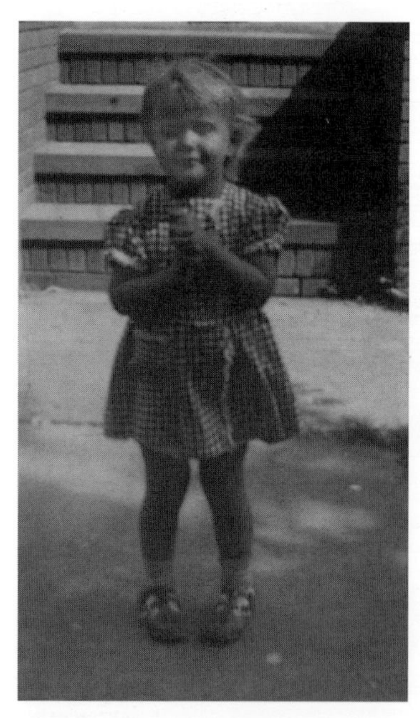

At two years and nine months of age, I am demonstrating the correct position for praying — eyes closed and hands clasped. Pigeon-toes optional.

Feisty and fearless, I was around ten here.

Susan and I in high school

Susan and I today

Newly divorced, "fat, stupid, and ugly" (according to my ex-husband) with my two children. These were hard times.

Pat and I just after we became engaged.

My husband, Pat, today. The second time around I picked a winner.

Our "Dream House." Finally!

interest in doctrinal disputes, will seriously suggest that it doesn't matter *which* god you believe in as long as you believe in *a* god. For sheer stupidity this assertion has few rivals. If belief in the Christian god and belief in the Muslim god and belief in a rain god named Bob are all equally valid, then all belief is silly and superfluous.

Belief in a supernatural being is not a prerequisite for humility or an awareness of the awesome beauty and power of nature. Humans can fully appreciate their puniness compared to the Cosmos, while at the same time appreciating man-made creations like music and humor. People can feel awe and reverence in the presence of death, and awe and joy at the moment of birth, without invoking higher powers. We can seek shelter from a destructive hurricane or appreciate the beauty of a comet progressing majestically across the sky without attributing it all to the whims of a capricious god.

Such beliefs may have served our ancestors in explaining such phenomena when the origin of even the gentlest rainfall was a truly baffling mystery. But even though meteorologists may still be wrong when predicting tomorrow's weather, we do finally understand, without a shadow of a doubt, that lightning bolts are not being hurled at us by displeased deities, nor are comets being sent to us by this same group to warn us of impending disaster. Reason, after all, has made some inroads.

Hopefully our great-great-grandchildren will never be exposed to the petulant, sadistic, imaginary gods invented by our superstitious, primitive ancestors, but rather to the almost limitless wonders and grandeur of our fascinating universe. With any luck our not-too-distant descendants, instead of wasting their precious intelligence worrying about whether or not a French kiss will send them to Hell, will be using their incredible powers of reason to explore this magnificent universe and to unravel the beckoning secrets of our own DNA. Our species is worthy of such a future. And if we can redirect our energies away from "Holy Wars," and stop frightening, and thereby stifling the potential of, our young people with vengeful, cruel gods; and if we will recognize our humanity for what it truly is — something precious and rare — then perhaps, just perhaps, such a glorious future awaits.

10

A Most Unlikely Freethinker

My Personal Journey

There was always music. My earliest memories are of music. I don't mean radio or phonograph albums, but our own, homegrown, family-generated music. My father was the pipe organist at church, my mother sang in the choir and occasionally on the radio (religious broadcasting only, of course) and we had an "upright grand" piano at home. I do miss the music.

My father, Edmund Meyer, was extremely gifted musically, as was my mother, LaVerne. Mom had a lovely, trained voice. Dad played the pipe organ brilliantly, often giving recitals, gave piano lessons, directed choir, and played organ or piano just for the sheer joy of it. And being a good sport, he always took requests. He could have been a professional musician, but was, instead, an executive with the Sherwin-Williams Paint Company.

I have only a few sketchy memories of our life in Lakewood, Ohio (just outside of Cleveland) because we moved to California when I was only four. Since I was so young when we moved, I never got to know all of my many aunts and uncles and cousins, and I'm sorry for that. Three of my grandparents had died before I was even born, so I never knew them either.

My paternal grandfather, Dr. John Meyer, would visit us every couple of years, and I wish I had had the chance to get to know him better. He had a remarkable life. The son of German immigrants (our whole clan was German), he became a Lutheran minister, and for several years was a missionary in South America. He could and did conduct church services in English, German, Spanish or Portuguese. He was also comfortable with Latin, Greek and Hebrew. He could read the Old Testament in its original Hebrew, and the New Testament in its original Greek. But my only memories of him are of a formal, dignified, aloof man, who always came to the dinner table wearing a suit and tie. Always. I never felt comfortable giggling around him. Or even smiling much, come to think of it.

The story goes that since he took his position as moral leader of his congregation so seriously, he insisted that all the window shades in his house be raised halfway, all day long until the lights were turned out, because there should be nothing going on in that house that was unfit for viewing by the public. I find that strange.

Anyway, the best record of our life in Ohio is not in the many great photographs, but in a priceless piece of wire. I managed to salvage one old wire recording that almost got thrown away on one of those hectic moving days. (Is there any other kind of moving day?) Most people don't even know what a wire recording is, but it predated tape recording by a bunch. Sound could be put on these spools of wire using a microphone, and then played back. Years ago we had that precious "Silvertone" wire recording transferred to tape, but it wasn't easy. My husband, Pat, had to go to a museum at Stanford University and beg the curator to allow him to *use* one of their wire recording machines that was on display. It was worth the begging.

Not at all surprising, the recording consists entirely of music. But what an array! There's Dad playing the piano, everything from college fight songs to Bach. There's Mom singing her lovely songs, accompanied by Dad. There's Dad playing the piano while a whole slew of my mother's relatives sing, in German, some German beer-hall numbers. The singers' enthusiasm outstrips their talent, and their enthusiasm was obviously enhanced by some good German beer, but it does sound like it was a fun evening. And then there is a lot of me and my older sister, Marilyn, making our bids for recording fame. I did a pretty good job on "Yittow Bodie In Da Twee," considering I wasn't even three. But "The Farmer In The Dell" goes on interminably, at a snail's pace, until you simply can't wait to get to that damn piece of cheese that stands alone.

I'm told that I was a strange toddler. Apparently I had a wonderful disposition, laughed a lot and was perfectly obedient from the outset. But, for the first two years of my life, I refused to talk. Unlike my older sister Marilyn who, around her first birthday, like normal humans, would repeat words in the normal fashion, and say "Ma-ma" and "ball" and "kitty," I simply stared intently at my mother as she tried to coax me to do the same thing. But she was wasting her time. I would have none of it.

My sister tried to cajole me as well, having a two-and-a-half-year edge on me, and not wanting her baby sister to look like an idiot. But I maintained my stubborn silence. I refused to repeat words, and by the time I was two my parents were really worried that something was wrong with me.

Then, shortly after my second birthday, I suddenly began speaking — in complete sentences. My first ever words were, "I wanna cuppa milk, pwease." Apparently my parents stared at me as if I had just stepped out of a flying saucer.

I find this very strange indeed, especially considering my love for the English language, which has been with me for as long as I can remember. There's an entry in my Baby Book where my mother wrote, quite bemused, that I wasn't even toilet-trained yet, but I constructed and uttered the compound sentence, "Marilyn goes to the toilet, but I tink in my pants." What a strange kid. Maybe I stared at my mother so intently, as she tried to get me to say doggie or something, because I was determined to figure out the whole language thing before I committed myself to the process. Well, I'll never know what that was all about. But my parents joked that after all the time that I refused to talk, once I began I never shut up.

Growing up in California should have been happier than it was, especially since my father had a wonderful job. My baby brother Robert had just joined the family (final total: two girls, one boy), and we lived in a beautiful neighborhood. But just before leaving Ohio, my poor mother became very ill. For two weeks her entire body was paralyzed. After her recovery, one side of her face remained permanently paralyzed, ruining her beautiful smile, and giving her a constantly watering eye. The official diagnosis by the single country doctor who attended her, was that she had Bell's Palsy. My father, however, believed she had polio, and I agree. Especially considering the time of her illness, 1949–1950, it seems most likely. I suppose it's also moot.

Dad said her health was never the same after that, and, sadly, I have too many memories of my mother lying on the couch or in bed, her medications always nearby. Oh, there were many happy memories, as my mother would read us stories, and sing with us around the piano, and joke and laugh, when she felt good. But that high-spirited, outgoing, lighthearted bundle of energy known as LaVerne Meyer ceased to exist before I even hit kindergarten. I would have loved to have met that woman.

On the brighter side, I actually liked school, got good grades, made friends easily, learned I had a good singing voice and joined any choir around. When not in school, there was usually a skate key around my neck, and since we lived in a very hilly neighborhood, skating was serious business. We're talking about some thirty-degree hills here. I was a daredevil on the monkey bars, and would scare the life out of my parents when I performed my feats, so I usually performed with no adult audience. Why I didn't kill myself is a mystery. I even used to borrow a boy's "Flexi," which is nothing more than a few slats of wood on four small wheels, about six inches off the ground, and I'd lie face down on it and race down our incredible hills. A Flexi was really just an accident looking for an exact location. I was fearless. Or stupid. Or both.

The neighborhood gang played baseball in the street (that was when traffic was almost nonexistent), and I remember that the concrete water-meter lid was first base. We played coed, boys and girls together, because there just weren't enough of either of the sexes to field its own team. Necessity precluded sexism. I was a pretty good hitter. In the summer we'd play until it was so dark we could barely see the ball, at which time we all also developed hearing problems as our various mothers called for us to come in. I also enjoyed basketball, and was a good forward. But swimming was another story. I still think that any body of water over four-and-a-half feet deep should be avoided by humans.

Shortly after getting the hang of this reading and writing stuff, I organized a small group of us into an editorial staff and founded *The Santa Ray News,* our only neighborhood newspaper. Writing is in my blood. "Santa Ray" was the name of the street we all lived on. I still have an old, yellowed copy of one of the issues, and its most notable feature is its surprisingly boring nature. We were not exactly Ace reporters. "The Cliffords got a new dog yesterday." Yawn. Of course, what do you want for three cents?

When I was twelve I fell in love with Elvis Presley, and my diary was filled with him. I always kept a diary and loved writing in it. I still have my photo album with pictures of Elvis lovingly glued to its pages. Then when I was twelve-and-a-half I fell in love with my English teacher, Mr. Ingmire, and Elvis had to share my diary pages with him. I still have some guilt pangs over being fickle. But love is a complicated business when you're twelve.

I'm also part of the generation that was truly dedicated to "The Mickey Mouse Club." I can still sing their opening and closing songs, and I remember that Tuesday was Guest Star Day. I also, like half of the country's youngsters, thought Annette Funicello was the coolest Mouseketeer imaginable. I couldn't wait till I could start growing breasts like hers. I look at her picture today (yes, I still have the 8 x 10 glossy of her that I paid fifty cents for) and wonder what all the fuss was about. But she was knocking us dead in the '50s.

During the summers, in grammar school, a bunch of us always went to the Wednesday afternoon matinees at the Grand Lake Theater. I was the only one who *hated* Ju-Ju Beads. But I could tolerate Milk Duds, and adored popcorn. I saw more Westerns and World War II movies than was probably healthy, but I loved them all. My anger and frustration knew no bounds, however, when, during the inevitable cowboy, barroom fight over a "girl," the girl just stood there, looking beautiful and worried, but saying and doing *nothing*. I wanted to shout at the screen, "Why don't you just tell them which guy you like best and then they won't have to fight!?" Why did the woman always act so stupid? Didn't she have any say in the matter? Would she just automatically belong to the guy who won the fight? That always ticked me off. I guess I was a nine-year-old feminist.

Christmases were always fun in our household, because my beloved Aunt Care (Caroline, my mother's sister) *always* came out to California from Ohio, and because my mother was a great cook. I swear she could have made gravy from a piece of shoe leather. And, naturally, there was always so much happy music. We'd stand around the piano and sing carols by the hour. I was also happy about my privileged status as a Missouri Synod Lutheran, since I knew Heaven awaited me and not everyone could make that claim.

My entire youth was church-oriented. Aside from the obvious Sunday service, there was also Sunday School before the service. I was in Junior Choir when I was young and Senior Choir later. There was choir practice on Thursday evenings, and "Confirmation" class every Saturday morning for two years, between ages eleven and thirteen. Every summer there were three weeks of Vacation Bible School, and every Christmas and Easter included pageants and all the accompanying rehearsals. In reading this list now, the word "indoctrination" rather than "teaching," springs to mind.

For me, though, there was even more. On Saturdays I would join my father in the choir loft, as he practiced the organ pieces for Sunday's service. I loved music, so I loved tagging along with him. He encouraged me to sing, and often I would stand in the balcony of Grand Lake Lutheran Church and sing my heart out, accompanied by Dad, as we both praised our Lord. (I can still sing most of the Lutheran liturgy from memory.) I also sang many solos in the church choir. I was a happy Christian.

Then, in the seventh grade, I met Susan Tanaka. We became best friends instantly, and are still best friends. Not being racist in any way, I barely noticed that she was Japanese. But when I learned that she was Buddhist, my world collapsed around me. I can still, today, remember my shock and horror (as if I had just met Godzilla) and then my fear. For I realized that my best friend, Susan, was going to Hell.

This, of course, was when my religious questions began. I had always asked questions about everything else under the sun, often exasperating my parents. This led to the common saying in our household, "Well, that's another *Judy*-Question." (Meaning difficult to answer.) But I had never questioned my religion. I knew it was the right one, and that's all there was to it. Then Susan came along. Now what?

I never did stop the religious questions until my faith had left completely, which is the inevitable result of serious, intelligent questioning. Interestingly, I can't remember the exact date, or even the exact year, when I finally realized I was an atheist. It was a long and painful transition for me. But I was somewhere in my mid- to late-twenties. This was the time period when I decided to, and did, read the entire Bible, in order to shore up my eroding faith. And, quite obviously, just the opposite happened. But it wasn't until then, when I realized at last that religion is simply part myth and part wishful thinking, that I finally stopped worrying about Susan.

In the meantime, I had made a tragic, life-ruining decision. I got married. Unfortunately, this marriage took place during my I'm-a-good-little-Christian-girl phase, when I knew that I must "obey" my husband and that my only real purpose in life was to breed many more little Christians. The birth of my first child, however, included eighteen hours of labor, and "many" was removed from my plans, Christian or no Christian. I ended up with one daughter, Deborah, and one son, Robert.

But my marriage was a shambles from the start, and I knew in those first couple of years that there was no hope. I, the former, feisty nine-year-old feminist, actually ironed my husband's *underwear,* briefs and T-shirts. He insisted. And I, the good, little Christian wife, obeyed. There were countless other indignities I endured, but I think the ironed underpants more or less tell the whole story. The life was being crushed out of me.

Although the divorce was painful, I knew I had to do it. I can pretty well sum up that marriage in one sentence: By the end of my marriage, my husband had positively convinced me that I was (a) stupid, (b) ugly and (c) fat. Looking back, it's difficult to understand how I could ever have viewed myself that way, but my husband had done a thorough job. (I was 5'7" tall and weighed 123 pounds.) If I had to rate my self-esteem at that time, on a scale of one to ten, I'd have to assign a negative number to it. It took me a long time to crawl out of that shell and think of myself as something not subhuman. I had always been a writer, but my husband didn't like my doing it ("girls" were supposed to be housewives only) and I had to hide what I did write. Ultimately I threw most of my writings away, to my eternal regret. But feelings of worthlessness make people do strange things.

Out on my own, then, with two small children, I floundered. With no self-confidence at all, I flitted here and there, looking for a man to provide me with an identity, since I didn't have one of my own. Those were tough times. I got a well-paying job with the phone company, but I hated it, and the commute was a killer. I did find a kind, loving man who loved me very much. But he was married. Just what I needed. More problems.

Then, in one of life's bizarre twists, I met my current husband, Pat. How did we meet? I love to tell this story because it's so unusual and could probably only happen in California. We had the same divorce lawyer. As anyone who has ever been divorced knows, the paperwork involved seems to go on forever, often lasting longer than the marriage being dissolved. Anyway, my lawyer knew that I was unhappy and that I worked for the phone company, and that I lived in Castro Valley, a small suburb in the San Francisco Bay Area. He had another client, Pat Hayes, who had just gone through a divorce, was also unhappy, worked for the phone company, and lived in Castro Valley. I was told that this Pat was a very nice man, and was just one year older than I. Would I like an introduction? And the rest, as they say, is history.

You know, it's amazing what love can do for a marriage. I mean the kind of love where the woman and the man are equal partners, joyfully celebrating the sexual aspect of human nature, helping each other through the rough spots, and just being silly together. I never knew that kind of love before I met Pat. And when we reached our fifteenth wedding anniversary and realized we were still having a whole lot of fun together, we sent a glowing thank-you note to our divorce lawyer!

After my two children had been launched safely into adulthood (one as a secretary with a large corporation and one as a computer-chip engineer in Silicon Valley) Pat and I purchased eighteen acres of land on top of a gorgeous hill out in the middle of nowhere. It isn't the end of the world, but you *can* see it from there. We needed to get away. Having both spent almost all of our lives in the San Francisco Bay Area, we were weary of the dirty air, crowded conditions and traffic snarl-ups. I commuted to San Francisco for some time, and I firmly believe that anyone dumb enough to run out of gas on the Bay Bridge during rush hour should be subject to the death penalty. (You can see that we needed to get away.)

Moreover, we had just passed through that stage of life known as "raising teenagers," a hair-raising, hair-graying task that makes the hazards of lion taming or mountain climbing pale by comparison. Fortunately, Pat had enough years with Pacific Bell to get a transfer to our "nowhere." Even "nowhere" needs phones. (Pat works with digital switching computers, and fiber optics and stuff like that. In other words, I don't understand a thing he does.) We were going to build our dream house. And we did. Literally.

Pat did most of the framing, and all of the plumbing, wiring, roofing, and painting with no one to help him but me. Yes, he is a master of all trades. It was quite a project. And Pat was working full-time while we did it. I kept the books and handled all of the money matters, and Pat would sometimes try to hide from me when he'd see me approaching with some invoices in my hand, and a questioning look on my face. We slogged away at this project for four of the longest years of our lives.

But strangely enough, though such house-building projects can actually cause divorces, Pat and I only grew closer. The building inspectors couldn't believe it. They said that they had expected to find Pat on his own, with me long gone, less than halfway through such a long building project. But I think that Pat and I realized how much we were *both* sacrificing for our dream home, and we tried to cheer each other up when either of us would get discouraged, which happened often. Fortunately our spells of total dejection ("This will never work. What the hell do we think we're doing?") rarely coincided.

The result? We have our dream house on top of our beautiful hill, with a view of two lakes, and a panorama of the Sierra Nevada foothills. And we know it is all the result of our own efforts. And we would never do it again in a million years. I get tired just thinking about it. Pat gets the hives. But we *are* happy here. Why did we build our own home in the first place? Well, we knew what we wanted and we knew what we could afford, and somehow the two didn't quite match.

And now, today, as I look back on my life, I see two distinct chapters, one religious and one secular. I also see, in myself, two completely different people in those two chapters. In the first part of my life, which was totally dominated by religion, I was frightened. I was terrified of going to Hell. I was afraid that if I really screwed up somehow, I would spend eternity suffering in Hell. This was a genuine, tangible fear for me. I agonized over it in my youth, contemplating the tortures that would be visited upon sinners in that very real place called Hell. My young, vivid imagination conjured up graphic, grisly scenarios that terrified me, scenarios involving fire, boiling oil and flesh being pierced with pitchforks. My hideous fears would sometimes keep me awake at night. I was obsessed with Hell.

Remembering what I went through in those early Christian years, I realize now that to instill such appalling fears in a child is a horrid thing to do. It's difficult to understand how loving parents can terrify their children this way with threats of Hell.

But it's still a common practice. And a cruel one.

As I grew up, and my fears of Hell became crystallized, my self-esteem and confidence slowly eroded. I worried that every mistake I made might be held against me on that inevitable Judgment Day. The only reason my disastrous first marriage took its course was that I had been properly programmed to accept, meekly, my lowly status as a female. Eve had sinned, and so my life was going to be crummy. Astonishingly, it made perfect sense to me at the time. And though I was never battered during that marriage, I was never struck, I can honestly say I don't know how I would have reacted if I had been — a most painful and disturbing admission.

The second part of my life, when I finally became a freethinker, was literally like being let out of prison. Of course my brain *had* been in shackles, fettered by superstitions and fears that stifle all intellectual inquiry. As a freethinker, I allowed my brain to come out of the closet, so to speak. I devoured books with a vengeance. I read books about freethought, evolution, cosmology, paleoanthropology, and so on, all books that would have been forbidden in my earlier life. And slowly, as my horizons broadened, I realized how my religion had warped my understanding of the entire universe around me.

Thus, when I finally broke free, I was like a butterfly newly emerged from the chrysalis. I was free to think, free to speak, free to act. I was *free.* It was a glorious awakening. And with the inevitable increase in self-esteem that accompanies genuine freethought, I discovered, to my surprised delight, that I was not fat, stupid and ugly. My outlook was forever changed, and I basked in the glow of my newfound confidence.

My new life as a freethinker allows me to see the entire world in a different light. Thinking for myself at last, I can see that the suffering millions in the Third World need bread, clean water and antibiotics, not prayers. I recognize the dreadful waste as precious resources are devoted to building churches instead of feeding the hungry. And I finally understand, clearly, that there is no such thing as a "holy" war.

Since my enlightenment, I have been accused of promoting a selfish "religion," humanism. But the bogus claim that humanism is a religion is a desperate attempt on the part of True Believers (a) to classify everyone as belonging to some sort of belief system and (b) to try to claim that if you teach humanism in school you must also teach other religions as well. "Equal time" stuff.

But how can anyone honestly claim that the *absence* of a belief in something is a religion? No one can, because it isn't. I don't believe in a deity, true. But I don't believe in Magic Elves, either. Does the absence of a belief in Magic Elves also constitute a "religion?" Humanism is no more a religion than the absence of a belief in leprechauns, elves or Santa Claus is a religion. Humanism is simply the affirmation of the fact that we have only our own humanity to rely on in our quest for a better world. I'm a humanist, but I certainly don't worship humanity. Clear-eyed at last, I worship nothing.

So then, my transition from Missouri Synod Lutheran to freethinking humanist has been quite a journey. While I sometimes feel a sense of poignant regret for all the years I lost to religion, I seldom look back. Instead, I celebrate the fact that I am no longer hamstrung by the oppressive ties of religion. At last I can fully experience, and appreciate, my own humanity. It was a long and arduous journey, but I can finally say, with a joyous certainty, that I am well and truly free.

Even as I write these words, I am gazing out at the lovely foothills surrounding me, and I realize how lucky I am to have such a breathtaking view on a daily basis. But so much more important, I know how fortunate I am to be able to share it all with such a special, loving, freethinking husband.

Bibliography

Asimov, Isaac, *Asimov's Guide to the Bible*, Avenel Books, New York, 1981.

Asimov, Isaac, *In the Beginning*, Crown Publishers, Inc., New York, 1981.

Attenborough, David, *Life on Earth*, Little, Brown and Company, Boston, 1979.

Barker, Dan, *Losing Faith In Faith: From Preacher To Atheist,* Freedom From Religion Foundation, Inc., 1992.

Basil, Robert and Gehrman, Mary Beth and Madigan, Tim, editors, *On the Barricades: Religion and Free Inquiry in Conflict*, Prometheus Books, New York, 1989.

Dakin, Edwin Franden, *Mrs. Eddy*, Charles Scribner's Sons, New York, 1930.

Darwin, Charles, *The Origin of Species*, The Crowell-Collier Publishing Company, 1962.

De Rosa, Peter, *Vicars of Christ*, Corgi Books, London, 1988.

Frazer, James G., *The Golden Bough*, Gramercy Books, New York, 1993 edition.

Gaylor, Annie Laurie, *Woe To The Women: The Bible Tells Me So,* Freedom From Religion Foundation, Inc., 1981.

Green, Ruth Hurmence, *The Born Again Skeptic's Guide To The Bible,* Freedom From Religion Foundation, Inc., 1979.

Helms, Randel, *Gospel Fictions*, Prometheus Books, New York, 1988.

Johanson, Donald and Edey, Maitland, *Lucy*, Warner Books, New York, 1981.

Larson, Orvin, *American Infidel: Robert G. Ingersoll,* Freedom From Religion Foundation, Inc., 1993.

Larue, Gerald A., *Ancient Myth and Modern Life*, Centerline Press, Long Beach, 1988.

Leakey, Richard E. and Lewin, Roger, *People of the Lake*, Anchor Press/Doubleday, New York, 1978.

McCollum, Vashti, *One Woman's Fight,* Freedom From Religion Foundation, Inc., 1993.

McGowan, Chris, *In the Beginning*, Prometheus Books, New York, 1984.

Morgan, Elaine, *The Aquatic Ape*, Stein and Day, New York, 1984.

Plaidy, Jean, *The Spanish Inquisition*, Barnes & Noble Books, New York, 1994.

Ranke-Heinemann, Uta, *Eunuchs For the Kingdom of Heaven: Women, Sexuality and the Catholic Church*, Doubleday, New York, 1990

Remsberg, John E., *The Christ*, Prometheus Books, New York, 1994.

Sagan, Carl, *Cosmos*, Random House, New York, 1980.

Schonfield, Hugh J., *The Passover Plot*, Bantam Books, Inc., New York, 1965.

Smith, George H., *Atheism: The Case Against God*, Prometheus Books, 1989.

Smith, Morton and Hoffmann, R. Joseph, editors, *What the Bible Really Says*, Prometheus Books, 1989.

Stone, Merlin, *When God Was a Woman*, Dorset Press, New York, 1976.

Talbert, Charles H., editor, *Reimarus: Fragments*, Fortress Press, Philadelphia, 1970.

Tierney, Patrick, *The Highest Altar: The Story of Human Sacrifice*, Viking Penguin, Inc., New York, 1989.

Time-Life Books, *Empires Ascendant*, (TimeFrame 400 BC – AD 200), Alexandria, Virginia, 1987.

Van Lawick-Goodall, Jane, *In the Shadow of Man*, Houghton Mifflin Company, Boston, 1971.

Wells, G.A., *Did Jesus Exist?*, (Revised Edition), Pemberton, London, 1986.

Wells, G.A., *The Historical Evidence for Jesus*, Prometheus Books, New York, 1988.

King James Version - *Holy Bible*

Chapter Notes

Chapter 3 - The Good Book

In "A Killing Update," the observation attributed to General Norman Schwarzkopf came from a David Frost interview with him that aired on PBS television station KVIE, Channel 6, in Sacramento, California, on March 27, 1991.

Chapter 4 - The Genesis of Absurdity

In "When It Rains, It Pours," the approximate date of the biblical Flood was taken from estimates made by Isaac Asimov in his book, *Asimov's Guide to the Bible*, Avenel Books, New York, 1981.

Chapter 5 - Sex and Satan

In "Here Comes The Bride," the information about the Roman Catholic Church and its position regarding sexuality was taken from Uta Ranke-Heinemann's book, *Eunuchs For the Kingdom of Heaven: Women, Sexuality and the Catholic Church.* (Doubleday, New York, 1990.) She is a most insightful theologian and her work is scholarly, detailed and highly informative.

Chapter 6 - The Messiah

In "The 'Christ-Killers'?" the many pagan and Jewish writers listed, who were all writing near the time of Jesus' supposed life, came from John E. Remsberg's *The Christ.* (Prometheus Books, New York, 1994.) Originally published by The Truth Seeker Company in 1909, *The Christ* is a consummate examination of every aspect of the supposed life of Jesus Christ.

The many anti-Semitic words and actions of various Popes may be found in Peter de Rosa's *Vicars of Christ.* (Corgi Books, London, 1988.) A most difficult book to find, it would be worth the effort for anyone interested in the real history of the papacy. De Rosa, the Dean of Theology at Corpus Christi College in London for six years, offers a devastating look at the evil that has been done for centuries in the name of the Pope.

All biblical quotations are taken from the King James Version of the Bible.

Index

C

D

E

F

K

L

M

Z